Mechanisms of Age-Cognition Relations in Adulthood

Mechanisms of Age-Cognition Relations in Adulthood

Timothy A. Salthouse
Georgia Institute of Technology

LAWRENCE ERLBAUM ASSOCIATES, PUBLISHERS
1992   Hillsdale, New Jersey   Hove and London

153
S177m

Lawrence Erlbaum Associates, Inc., Publishers
365 Broadway
Hillsdale, New Jersey 07642

Library of Congress Cataloging-in-Publication Data

Salthouse, Timothy A.
      Mechanisms of age–cognition relations in adulthood / Timothy A.
      Salthouse.
            p.   cm. — (John M. MacEachran memorial lecture series : 1991)
            Includes bibliographical references and index.
            ISBN 0–8058–1129–X
            1. Cognition—Age factors. 2. Memory—Age factors. 3. Adulthood—
      Psychological aspects. I. Title. II. Series.
      BF724.55.C63S22   1992
      153—dc20   92–10054
                                                                                    CIP

Printed in the United States of America
10 9 8 7 6 5 4 3 2 1

Contents

Preface   vii

John M. MacEachran Memorial Lecture   viii
Series

CHAPTER 1
The Phenomenon and the Methods to Be   1
Used in Its Investigation

The Age-Cognition Phenomenon   4
Importance of the Phenomenon   12
Assumptions and Biases   16
Method to Investigate Mechanisms   19
Statistical Control Procedures   21
Mediator Importance   24
Methodological Requirements of Statistical   26
    Control Procedures
Summary of Strategy   29
Types of Mediators   29
Process-Related Mediators   34

v

CHAPTER 2
Working Memory as a Potential Mediator   37

Measurement of Working Memory   40
Statistical Control Results   45
Manipulation of Working Memory Demands   48
Statistical Control Analyses of Simple and   59
    Complex Cognitive Tasks
Information Availability   61
Causes of Relations Between Age and   72
    Working Memory

CHAPTER 3
Processing Speed as a Potential Mediator   81

Age-Speed Relations   84
Selection of Best Measure of Speed   88
Statistical Control of Speed   93
How Does Slower Speed of Processing   99
    Affect Quality of Cognitive Performance?
Refining the Nature of the Speed Mediator   100
Perceptual or Motor Speed?   111
Further Decomposition of Speed?   115

CHAPTER 4
Summary   117

Directions for Future Research   121
Concluding Comments   123

References   125
Author Index   129
Subject Index   131

Preface

This monograph is the written version of a series of talks delivered as the 1991 MacEachern Lectures at the University of Alberta. The informal style of the lectures, and the inclusion of a relatively large number of figures, has been preserved in order to keep the monograph faithful to the concept of an individual describing his own research. I viewed the lecture series as an opportunity to integrate the results of my research over the last 5 years into a single, reasonably coherent, framework. The monograph thus is very much a personal account of one individual's perspective and research, although the studies reported are naturally a product of many collaborations, and of inspirations from numerous colleagues.

I would like to acknowledge financial support from the National Institute on Aging through Grants AG06826 and AG06858 that made the research described in this monograph possible. I also want to thank Professors Neil Charness and Robert Kail for their thoughtful critiques of a draft of this monograph, the faculty and students at the University of Alberta for their stimulating questions and comments regarding the lectures, and the graduate students in the Cognitive Aging Program at the Georgia Institute of Technology for providing feedback on several of the ideas discussed in this monograph as they were in the process of being developed.

Timothy A. Salthouse

John M. MacEachran Memorial Lecture Series

The Department of Psychology at the University of Alberta in-augurated the MacEachran Memorial Lecture Series in 1975 in honor of the late John M. MacEachran. Professor MacEachran was born in Ontario in 1877 and received a Ph.D. in Philosophy from Queen's University in 1905. In 1906 he left for Germany to begin more formal study in psychology, first spending just less than a year in Berlin with Stumpf, and then moving to Leipzig, where he completed a second Ph.D. in 1908 with Wundt as his supervisor. During this period he also spent time in Paris studying under Durkheim and Henri Bergson. With these impressive qualifications the University of Alberta was par-ticularly fortunate in attracting him to its faculty in 1909.

Professor MacEachran's impact has been significant at the univer-sity, provincial, and national levels. At the University of Alberta he offered the first courses in psychology and subsequently served as Head of the Department of Philosophy and Psychology and Provost of the University until his retirement in 1945. It was largely owing to his activities and example that several areas of academic study were established on a firm and enduring basis. In addition to playing a major role in establishing the Faculties of Medicine, Education and Law in the Province, Professor MacEachran was also instrumental in the formative stages of the Mental Health Movement in Alberta. At a national level, he was one of the founders of the Canadian Psychologi-cal Association and also became its first Honorary President in 1939. John M. MacEachran was indeed one of the pioneers in the develop-ment of psychology in Canada.

Perhaps the most significant aspect of the MacEachran Memorial Lecture Series has been the continuing agreement that the Department of Psychology at the University of Alberta has with Lawrence Erlbaum Associates, Publishers, Inc., for the publication of each lecture series. The following is a list of the Invited Speakers and the titles of their published lectures:

1975	Frank A. Geldard (Princeton University) "Sensory Saltation: Mestastability in the Perceptual World"
1976	Benton J. Underwood (Northwestern University) "Temporal Codes for Memories: Issues and Problems"
1977	David Elkind (Rochester University) "The Child's Reality: Three Developmental Themes"
1978	Harold Kelley (University of California at Los Angeles) "Personal Relationships: Their Structures and Processes"
1979	Robert Rescorla (Yale University) "Pavlovian Second-Order Conditioning: Studies in Associative Learning"
1980	Mortimer Mishkin (NIMH–Bethesda) "Cognitive Circuits" (*unpublished*)
1981	James Greeno (University of Pittsburgh) "Current Cognitive Theory in Problem Solving" (*unpublished*)
1982	William Uttal (University of Michigan) "Visual Form Detection in 3-Dimensional Space"
1983	Jean Mandler (University of California at San Diego) "Stories, Scripts, and Scenes: Aspects of Schema Theory"
1984	George Collier and Carolyn Rovee-Collier (Rutgers University) "Learning and Motivation: Function and Mechanism" (*unpublished*)
1985	Alice Eagly (Purdue University) "Sex Differences in Social Behavior: A Social-Role Interpretation"
1986	Karl Pribram (Stanford University) "Brain and Perception: Holonomy and Structure in Figural Processing"
1987	Abram Amsel (University of Texas at Austin) "Behaviorism, Neobehaviorism, and Cognitivism in Learning Theory: Historical and Contemporary Perspectives"
1989	Robert S. Siegler and Eric Jenkins (Carnegie Mellon University) "How Children Discover New Strategies"
1991	Timothy A. Salthouse (Georgia Institute of Technology) "Mechanisms of Age–Cognition Relations in Adulthood"

Eugene C. Lechelt, Coordinator
MacEachran Memorial Lecture Series

Sponsored by The Department of Psychology, The University of Alberta with the support of The Alberta Heritage Foundation for Medical Research in memory of John M. MacEachran, pioneer in Canadian psychology.

Chapter 1
The Phenomenon and the Methods to Be Used in Its Investigation

I begin by describing two important restrictions on the material covered in this monograph. The first is that I refer only to my own research. This does not mean that I am unaware of, or unappreciative of, the important contributions of others. I firmly believe that progress in science is accomplished because of the combined efforts of a great many people, and thus a personal perspective inevitably provides a distorted portrayal of the total knowledge in a field, and of how that knowledge was achieved. Nevertheless, it is sometimes interesting to examine an individual researcher's approach to a problem, and it is certainly easier for that individual to describe his or her own research than also to attempt to review and integrate the research of others. Moreover, this type of egocentric perspective may be defensible when, as in the present case, almost all of the research to be discussed has been described in journal articles where the relevant research of other investigators has been cited.

The second restriction on the scope of the discussion is that it is limited to what is known as fluid or process aspects of cognition. That is, the focus is on the efficiency or effectiveness of processing at the time of evaluation, and not on the accumulated products of prior processing or inventories of one's knowledge. The emphasis is therefore on what Horn and Cattell (1967) refer to as *fluid intelligence,* rather than what they term *crystallized intelligence,* and on measures like those in the WAIS–R (Wechsler, 1981) Performance scale instead of those in the WAIS–R Verbal scale. The reason for this restriction is very pragmatic—these are the measures that have been found to have the largest relations with age, and consequently are the most in need of explanation.

The major issue to be addressed in this monograph is represented in Figure 1.1, and can be succinctly expressed in the form of the

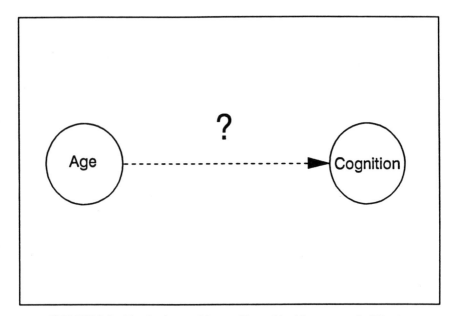

FIGURE 1.1   The fundamental issue addressed in this monograph: What is responsible for the relations between age and cognition?

following question: What is responsible for the relations between age and measures of cognitive functioning? More specifically, the purpose of this monograph is to describe the research I have conducted in which I have attempted to replace the question mark with detailed mechanisms.

THE AGE–COGNITION PHENOMENON

An important initial step is to describe the phenomenon to be explained. The research participants in the projects I discuss were primarily middle class adults, with moderately high levels of education (typically averaging between 14 and 15 years of formal education), who generally reported themselves to be in good to excellent health. In most of the projects I have tried to obtain nearly the same number of males and females, and the age range of the participants usually has been between about 18 and 80 years of age. These characteristics mean that I am not dealing with the very old, or with individuals obviously suffering from debilitating diseases. Instead, I am concerned with normal aging across a wide range of adulthood, and not extreme old age or pathological aging. Most research participants were recruited from newspaper advertisements, community organizations, and referrals from other participants. Some of the projects involved two extreme groups, in which case the young adults typically were students (almost always between 18 and 25 years of age), and the older adults were volunteers from the community (usually between 55 and 80 years of age).

A wide range of tests or tasks were used to assess cognitive functioning in these projects. (The terms *tests* and *tasks* are used interchangeably in this monograph.) Three typical tests are illustrated in Figure 1.2. An example of a test used to measure reasoning abilities is the Raven's Advanced Progressive Matrices. As can be seen in the top panel of Figure 1.2, items in this test consist of a matrix of geometric patterns in eight cells of a 3×3 matrix. The requirement for the examinee is to select the best completion for the missing cell in the matrix from a set of eight alternative patterns.

The Paper Folding Test is an example of the type of test used to measure spatial abilities. The examinee in this test is to inspect a series of rectangles representing the folding of a piece of paper and the punching of a hole through the folded paper, and then to determine whether the displayed pattern of holes would result from that sequence of folds and punch location.

One test used to assess memory abilities is the Spatial Matrix Memory Test. The to-be-remembered material in this test consists of the locations of seven targets in a 5×5 matrix, and recall is evaluated in terms of the number of targets reproduced in their correct positions in a blank matrix.

Comparison of results across such different kinds tests is complicated when the measures are not in the same scale, and only indirect contrasts may be possible when the tests have different units of measurement. Moreover, direct comparisons are not always meaningful even when all the variables are reported in the same units. As an example, two tests might both be measured in terms of the percentage of responses answered correctly, but the measures may not be equivalent because the tasks might vary in the difficulty of the discriminations, or in the accuracy rates attributable to chance (e.g., 12.5% for the Raven's Progressive Matrices Test, and 50% for the Paper Folding Test).

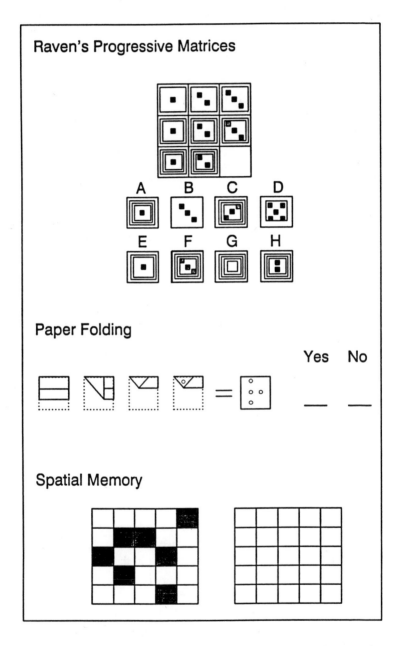

FIGURE 1.2 Examples of items in three cognitive tests assessing reasoning ability, spatial ability, and memory ability.

One method of avoiding the problem of disparate performance measures is to convert the performance measures into standard deviation units of young adults. This transformation leads to all measures having the same meaning because the new measurement scale refers to the relative position of the score in a reference distribution. That is, all scores can be interpreted in terms of the percentage of scores in the reference distribution above or below that value. Any of several different groups could be used as the reference group, but defining young adults as the reference group may provide the most sensitive evaluation of the age relations. Another possibility is to use the distribution from the entire sample as the reference group. The disadvantage of this procedure, however, is that the age relations will likely be underestimated because the standard deviation from the entire sample includes between-age as well as within-age variation.

Just as there are many ways to represent cognitive performance, there are also many ways to represent relations between age and performance. A particularly informative method consists of portraying the distribution of scores from the entire sample, and then the distributions for each successive decade. If age is systematically associated with level of performance, then one would expect a differentiation of the distributions according to age.

Distributions of scores in the total sample, and in each decade, for the three tests described earlier are illustrated in the next three figures. Figure 1.3 represents the data from 221 adults with the Raven's Advanced Progressive Matrices Test (Salthouse, 1991a, Study 1), Figure 1.4 represents the data from 383 adults on the Paper Folding Test (Salthouse & Mitchell, 1990), and Figure 1.5 represents the data from 362 adults on the Spatial Memory Test (Salthouse, Kausler, & Saults, 1988). The age relations in each figure are evident both in the gradual shift of the distributions toward lower scores with increased age, and in the progressively lower means (indicated by the arrows) at successive decades. These figures clearly indicate that the overall distribution can be decomposed into separate distributions distinguished by the age of the individual.

Partitioning of the variance in the total distribution can be quantified in terms of the proportion of variance, or R^2, associated with age in a regression equation predicting the measure of cognitive performance. The R^2 for the three measures represented in Figures 1.3, 1.4, and 1.5, and for five additional measures, are portrayed in Figure 1.6. The Venn

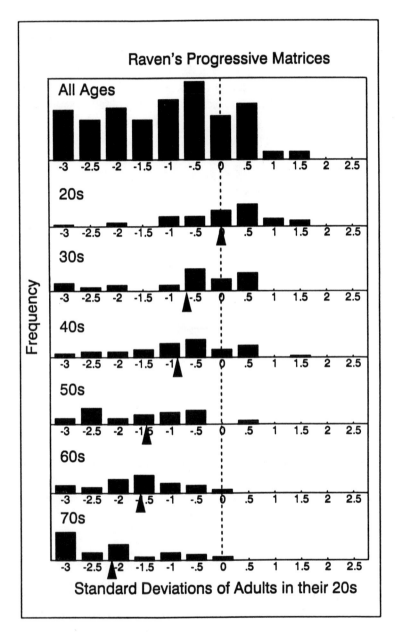

FIGURE 1.3   Distribution of Raven's Progressive Matrices scores, in young adult standard deviation units, across all ages and at each age decade. Data from Salthouse (1991a, Study 1).

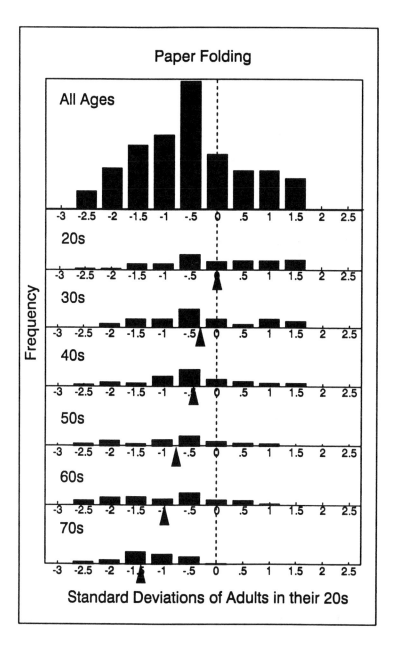

FIGURE 1.4   Distribution of Paper Folding scores, in young adult standard deviation units, across all ages and at each age decade. Data from Salthouse and Mitchell (1990).

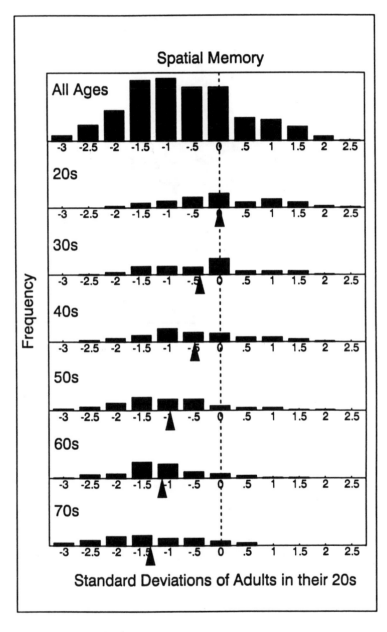

FIGURE 1.5 Distribution of Spatial Matrix Memory scores, in young adult standard deviation units, across all ages and at each age decade. Data from Salthouse, Kausler, and Saults (1988).

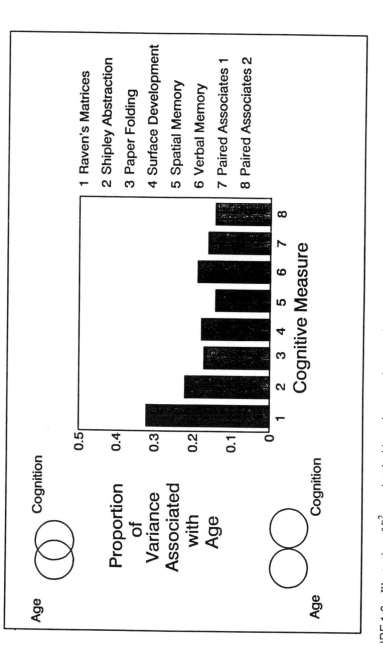

FIGURE 1.6   Illustration of R^2 associated with age in regression equations predicting cognitive performance. Data Sets 1 and 2 from Salthouse (1991a, Study 1), Sets 3 and 4 from Salthouse and Mitchell (1990), Sets 5, 6, and 7 from Salthouse, Kausler, and Saults (1988), and Set 8 from Salthouse (in preparation).

diagrams in the left of the figure illustrate that the R^2 values can be interpreted as representing the degree of overlap of the circle representing the age variance with the circle representing the cognition variance.

The results in this figure are fairly typical because R^2 values of between about .1 and .3 have been reported across a wide range of cognitive variables. The absolute proportion of the total variance in cognitive measures systematically related to age is rather small, but it is almost always significantly greater than zero, and is larger than most other single-variable influences on behavior. In support of this last point is Cohen's (1988) observation that correlations in the behavioral sciences are small if $r = .1$, medium if $r = .3$, and large if $r = .5$. Most of the relations represented in this figure, which correspond to the square of the correlation, therefore would be considered medium to large in the context of behavioral research.

The R^2 values derived from linear regression equations may underestimate the true magnitude of the association between age and measures of cognition if some of the relations are nonlinear. Although nonlinear trends are sometimes reported in data of this type, few quadratic or cubic trends were statistically significant in analyses of the data I describe, and even when significant they invariably were associated with very small increments in variance relative to the variance associated with the linear relation. It therefore seems reasonable to consider the relations between age and cognition as primarily linear in nature.

The same general pattern of a systematic association between adult age and cognitive performance has been reported in many different variables, including, but not restricted to, those assessing reasoning, spatial, and memory abilities. This pattern of negative relations between age and performance in a variety of cognitive assessments is the phenomenon addressed in this monograph.

IMPORTANCE OF THE PHENOMENON

There are several reasons to believe that age–cognition relations of the type just described could be important outside the research laboratory. One reason is that performance on similar cognitive measures has been found to be related to occupational level as well as to age. Both of these relations are apparent in Figure 1.7, which illustrates two

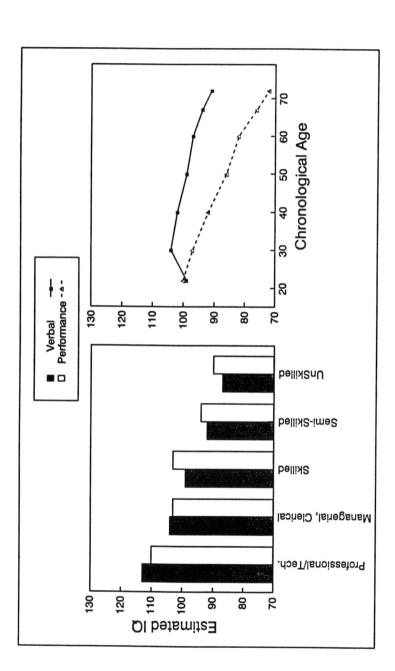

FIGURE 1.7 Mean Verbal and Performance IQs from the WAIS–R standardization sample as a function of occupational level and age. Occupational data from Kaufman (1990) and age data derived from values reported in Wechsler (1981).

analyses of the data from the WAIS–R standardization sample (data from Kaufman, 1990, and Wechsler, 1981). Of particular interest are the results with the Performance IQ measures because the tests comprising that scale are most similar to the fluid or process type of cognition of primary concern here. Notice that average Performance IQ differs by about 20 points from the highest to the lowest occupational level among adults between 20 and 54 years of age. This indicates that incumbents in occupations varying in status or prestige have substantially different average levels of cognitive performance. However, the figure additionally reveals that the difference in average performance between age 20 and age 70 on these same measures is nearly 30 points. The age-related variation with these measures of cognitive functioning is therefore greater than that found across major occupational categories.

Measures of cognitive performance also have been found to be associated with success in various jobs. For example, validity coefficients for cognitive measures in the prediction of job proficiency have been found to range between .25 and .45 (e.g., Ghiselli, 1973; Hunter & Hunter, 1984). Because of their established validity, measures of cognitive performance are often used for purposes of selection. And because increased age frequently is associated with lower levels of cognitive performance, dramatically different selection consequences could occur if the same absolute performance criteria were used for all groups. This point can be made more concrete by reference to Figure 1.8, which illustrates the percentages at the top and bottom 10% of the reference distribution in distributions that have been shifted towards lower levels of performance. Both ends of the distributions are represented because the bottom 10% might serve as the rejection region for some positions, and the top 10% might function as the selection region for other positions.

If, as the results illustrated in Figures 1.3, 1.4, and 1.5 suggest, the average adult in his or her 60s performs about 1 to 1.5 standard deviations below the average adult in his or her 20s, then he or she may be 4 to 6 times more likely to fall in the low rejection region, and only 1/9 to 1/50 as likely to fall in the high selection region. By virtually any standard, differences of this magnitude would be considered substantial.

I suspect that these kinds of measures of fluid or process cognition may be less important than acquired knowledge in predicting success

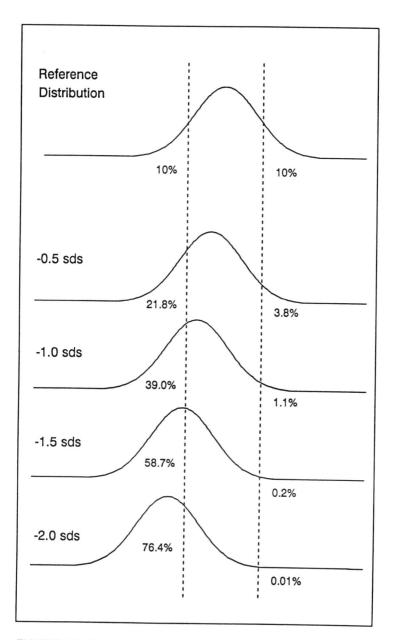

FIGURE 1.8   Illustration of percentages corresponding to the top and bottom 10% of a reference distribution in distributions shifted various amounts relative to the reference distribution.

in occupational situations as people accumulate experience and knowledge in a job. At the same time, however, I would also be surprised if fluid or process aspects of cognitive functioning were found to be completely independent of occupational success, particularly when performance is assessed on novel activities and in unfamiliar situations. This type of cognition therefore probably has at least some relevance for job performance at all stages of a career, and for many types of jobs.

All of the implications of the negative relations between age and certain measures of cognitive functioning are not yet understood. Nevertheless, because cognitive measures have been found to predict success in a variety of non-academic situations, the potential consequences of these relations could be great. Even if only for this reason, therefore, the phenomenon of negative relations between age and cognition appears important enough to justify serious efforts at explanation.

ASSUMPTIONS AND BIASES

All research is guided by numerous implicit assumptions or biases. Because they may help explain the particular approach I have adopted in attempting to determine the mechanisms responsible for age–cognition relations, I mention a few of the assumptions and biases that have influenced my choice of research issues and investigative methods. Many alternative sets of assumptions obviously could be used to guide one's research, and those described below are clearly not the only reasonable ones within the field of aging and cognition. I thus try to justify these particular assumptions by briefly describing the rationale or motivation underlying each assumption.

An initial assumption or bias is that the age differences in various cognitive measures are not completely independent of one another. A reflection of this bias is my belief that it is useful to postulate the existence of some commonalities in the causes of age relations across various measures of cognitive functioning instead of proposing unique, and independent, interpretations for every cognitive measure in which age differences have been reported. The latter strategy has been dominant over the last several decades, and in my opinion has led to a confusing and unintegrated literature (Salthouse, 1985b, 1988a,

1991b, in press-e). We eventually may find that separate and distinct explanations for each measure are necessary, but it is unlikely that any broader influences that might exist will be discovered if there are never any attempts to look for them. At least judging from current research practices, there seems to be considerable resistance to the idea that some age-related variance might be attributable to influences broader than the characteristics of specific tasks. My view is that this is a very interesting possibility that warrants careful investigation, and hence it should not be dismissed a priori, and on the basis of little or no evidence.

A second assumption is that the variance of greatest interest to developmental researchers is the variance in the dependent variable that is systematically related to age, and not the total variance in the dependent variable. In other words, I don't believe that developmental researchers should necessarily be attempting to account for all of the variance in measures of cognitive functioning because the goal of merely explaining that portion of the variance associated with age is itself quite ambitious. Only after moderate progress has been achieved in accounting for substantial proportions of the age-associated variance would it seem realistic to try to explain the variance associated with other factors.

This assumption has several implications for the types of analyses that should be conducted when investigating age–cognition relations. Perhaps the most fundamental is that steps should be taken to ensure that one is trying to explain merely that portion of cognitive behavior that has been found to be related to age. As is discussed later, this often requires that the researcher first identify the age-related variance, and then partition only this variance into different potential determinants.

Another important assumption is that some measures of cognitive functioning are more informative than others. This assumption implies that the selection of measures to be investigated should not be arbitrary, but rather should be based on clearly specified rational grounds. Two informal criteria have guided my choice of cognitive tasks. One is that the performance measure should have moderate to large age relations. Age-related effects may be large because the measure is susceptible to many distinct age-related influences, or because it is very sensitive to a primary aging factor. In either case, that measure is likely to be more informative about the causes of age-related influences than measures with smaller age relations.

The second criterion I have considered in the selection of tasks to be investigated is that the measure of cognitive functioning should have large relations with other cognitive measures. The justification for this criterion is a belief that age differences in one measure are important to the extent that they are informative about the age differences in other measures. That is, few age differences are inherently interesting by themselves because there are simply too many measures that could be investigated. The efficiency of research needs to be maximized by focusing on measures likely to have the greatest generality. Theoretical arguments could be used to defend the presumed centrality of a particular measure, but the speculations are most convincing when they are accompanied by empirical evidence (e.g., correlations, factor analyses, etc.) that the target measure actually is related to other cognitive measures.

A fourth assumption is that the greatest generality may be evident at a more abstract level of analysis than that represented by a measure of performance from a single cognitive task. According to psychometric theory, all measures can be assumed to reflect construct variance, method- or task-specific variance, and error variance. That is, performance measures are influenced by one or more theoretical constructs, by the particular tasks and methods used to assess performance, and by various types of errors. The variance of greatest interest, the construct variance, can be emphasized by aggregating across multiple measures of the construct to average out, either through cancellation or dilution, the variance associated with specific materials and procedures. Because the methods and materials used in any single assessment have less of an influence on an aggregate or composite variable based on several measures, inferences based on results from multiple measures can be expected to have greater generalizability than those based on results from single measures.

It is probably this aspect of my thinking about research methodology that has changed the most as I became more knowledgeable about psychometric methods. As an experimental psychologist I viewed my primary goal as the pursuit of precision, and consequently I often tried to narrow or refine the task to eliminate what I considered to be irrelevant variance. It is only in the last few years that I have fully appreciated the argument that purity frequently means specificity, which can in some circumstances lead to loss of generality. I have therefore come to believe that both analytical and aggregational approaches are needed, and consequently I probably am not as much of a methodological chauvinist as I once was.

For many of the analyses described, several measures have been combined to create a composite cognition measure. The composite thus represents aspects from all of the included measures, and particularly those aspects that the measures have in common. In effect, therefore, cognition is being treated as a meaningful higher-level construct. Of course, no single composite can be assumed to represent all of cognition, or even all of the fluid or process aspects of cognition. However, because it is cumbersome to create, and to use, distinct labels for composites based on different combinations of measures, for the sake of convenience I use the generic term *cognition* when referring to these composites based on multiple cognitive measures.

The composites discussed have been created by averaging z-scores (i.e., a unit-weighted, variance-adjusted, combination), rather than by more complicated techniques. This method of aggregation has limitations (e.g., the variables are assumed to be equally important, and the composites still include measurement error), but it is easier in the early stages of research to work with simple composites than with more abstract measures derived from elaborate procedures based on factor analysis and latent construct modeling.

A final assumption or bias influencing my approach to research is the belief that replication is essential to avoid premature theorizing. I find that I am much more impressed when important results are replicated, and efforts are directed toward explaining the pattern common to two or more independent studies, than when elaborate explanations are provided for even the smallest details of the results from a single study. Statisticians frequently note that cross-validation is needed to avoid capitalizing on chance, and it is for similar reasons that I believe that one can be confident that results are not sample specific only when the major findings have been replicated in an independent sample.

METHOD TO INVESTIGATE MECHANISMS

The focus of this monograph is on mechanisms responsible for age–cognition relations. The relations have been documented to exist, their potential importance has been briefly discussed, and some of my research biases have been identified. Let me now turn to how I propose to investigate possible mechanisms.

Age refers to an interval between two points in time. One point corresponds to the birth of the individual, and the other to the time of some relevant measurement. Age is therefore not a direct causal factor, but merely a dimension along which many factors could be exerting their influence. The goal in understanding age-related effects on cognition is to identify factors that reflect what is occurring over time, and then to examine the role each factor might have as a mediator of age–cognition relations.

A mediator can be defined as something interposed between two variables, and that is at least partially responsible for the relation between them. The effects of the first variable on the second are carried or transmitted through the mediator such that those effects would not occur to the same degree if the mediator had not been present. At least initially, mediators must be considered provisional because one can seldom be certain that the mediator is truly responsible for the relation between the two relevant variables. For example, other more fundamental mediators might intervene between one of the variables and the candidate mediator, or some additional factor might influence the relations among the hypothesized mediator and both variables. Nevertheless, research proceeds through a sequence of iterations, and hence the true status of suspected mediators can be expected to be revealed as relevant research results accumulate.

The identification of potential mediators is an important first step in understanding the mechanisms responsible for the relations between age and cognition. Once potential mediators have been identified, two complementary methods can be used to investigate the mechanisms. One method is that of statistical control. This method is particularly useful for establishing the existence of relations among age, measures of cognitive functioning, and the measures used as indexes of the hypothesized mediators. The second method is experimental analysis in which the processes responsible for the relations documented with statistical control procedures are investigated. That is, the goal with analytical procedures is to identify the mechanisms involved in the relations between age and the mediator, and between the mediator and the measures of cognition. The particular procedures will vary according to the nature of the hypothesized mediator, but the fundamental aim is always to specify how and why the relations occur.

STATISTICAL CONTROL PROCEDURES

The reasoning underlying the use of statistical control procedures to investigate the existence of relations among age, potential mediators, and cognition can be described with the aid of Figure 1.9. This figure illustrates three models of possible relations among these variables, with the relations portrayed both in the form of path diagrams, and in terms of Venn diagrams indicating shared variance. Model A illustrates the possibility of complete mediation in that all of the influence of age on cognition is channeled through the mediator. The situation of no true mediation is represented by model B. In this case, the suspected mediator is not really a mediator because the mediator–cognition relation is spurious in the sense that it only occurs because of the influence of age on both variables. Model C represents the possibility of partial mediation because there are both direct and indirect, or mediated, influences of age on cognition.

These alternatives can all be investigated by focusing on model C, and relying on the strength of specific relations to discriminate among the models. That is, model A implies that there should be no age–cognition relation after the mediator is controlled, and model B implies that there should be no mediator–cognition relation after age is controlled. Tests of whether these relations are zero therefore can be conducted in the context of analyses examining the simultaneous influence of both age and the mediator on cognition.

An ideal strategy for investigating the hypothesized relations might involve random assignment of individuals to groups in which both age and the level of the hypothesized mediator are independently varied. That is, the most desirable method of minimizing the influence of extraneous variables is to assign people randomly to the relevant groups. Unfortunately, age is not a manipulable variable, and manipulation of the level of a mediator is seldom practical, and possibly not ethical, with adult developmental research in which the relevant phenomena, and perhaps the operation of the mediator, extend for decades.

Another possible strategy would be to match people of different ages on an index of the mediator. In other words, if sufficiently large

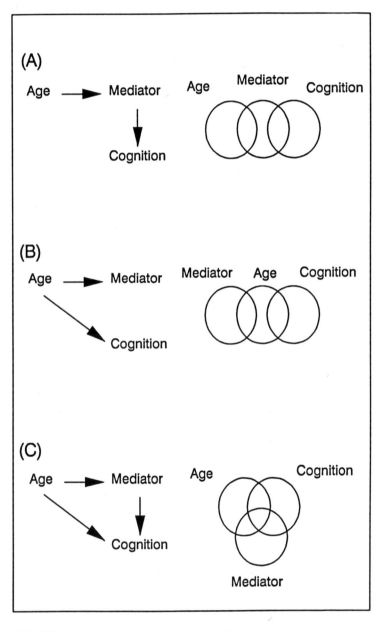

FIGURE 1.9 Three alternative models of the relations among age, cognition, and a mediator.

samples are available, it might be possible to find people of different ages with nearly identical values of the mediator. The expectation under conditions where there is no relation between age and the mediator is that, at least according to models A and C, the age differences in cognition would either be eliminated or substantially reduced. This approach also has problems, however, because statistical power is reduced when sample size is decreased by omitting the nonmatched individuals, and regression-to-the-mean artifacts may occur when people are selected from the extremes of the distributions of scores.

What seems to be the most feasible method for investigating hypothesized relations among age, cognition, and possible mediators involves the use of statistical control procedures. These techniques essentially equate people artificially, by using statistical methods to remove the linear influence of the hypothesized mediator from the measure of cognition. Of course there is no assurance that individuals equated on the level of the mediator are equivalent in other respects, but results from what are essentially correlational procedures can nonetheless be very informative even if they do not permit strong inferences about cause–effect relations.

Statistical control procedures are based on a number of assumptions. Some of these, such as linearity of the relations between variables, and equivalence of the mediator–cognition relations at different ages, can be investigated with appropriate analyses of the data. However, other assumptions are not as easily examined. An example is the assumption that the consequences of a particular level of a mediator are equivalent regardless of the etiology or developmental history of the mediator (Salthouse, 1991b). To illustrate, if one were to focus on health status as a potential mediator, it is assumed that the current level of health has the same influence on cognitive functioning whether it is a consequence of a long gradual decline, or of a sudden illness.

This assumption may not be completely realistic because of the possibility of adaptations to the initial alteration such that the consequences differ depending on the time course of the mediator. For instance, suppose level of vision is the mediator under investigation, and that a measure of visual acuity is used as the index of vision. The implicit assumption with statistical control procedures is that a gradual loss of vision that has occurred over many years in a 60-year-old is equivalent to a congenital condition of low vision in a 40-year-old, and to an accident-induced partial blindness found in a 20-year-old. The manner in which the mediator is operationally defined can obviously be refined, but as long as the assumption of irrelevant etiology is not examined, caution must be exerted in interpreting the results of statistical control procedures when they are used to investigate mediators of age–cognition relations.

MEDIATOR IMPORTANCE

In most of the analyses based on statistical control procedures that I have conducted, I have relied on multiple regression procedures to estimate the importance of hypothesized mediators. The relevant comparisons are the age-related variance (in the form of squared semipartial correlations) before and after the linear influence of the mediator has been removed. In the context of these procedures, the importance of the mediator is directly related to the degree to which the age-related variance is reduced when the mediator is controlled. Statistical significance is of secondary concern because the primary goal is to estimate the magnitude of various influences, and not simply to determine whether a particular influence is significantly greater than zero.

The rationale underlying the evaluation of the importance of a mediator to the age–cognition relations can be clarified by reference to Figure 1.10. The shaded columns in the left of the figure represent the proportion of variance in the cognitive variable associated with age. In terms of the Venn diagrams, this column corresponds to the proportion of the circle representing cognition variance that overlaps with the circle representing age variance. The unfilled columns in the left of Figure 1.10 indicate the proportion of age-related variance in the cognitive variable that remains after removing the linear influence of the hypothesized mediator. If the mediator is weak, then the residual age-related variance will be large, as portrayed in the top panel of the figure, and if the mediator is strong, then the residual variance will be small, as represented in the bottom panel. The Venn diagrams indicate that weak mediation corresponds to a small region in which age, cognition, and mediator all overlap, whereas strong mediation corresponds to a large region in which the three variables overlap.

Results from the types of analyses just described can be expressed in terms of the difference between the initial and the residual age-re-

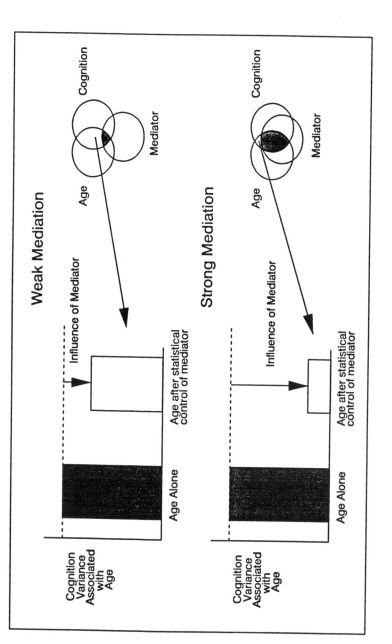

FIGURE 1.10   Illustration of weak and strong mediation of age–cognition relations.

lated variance divided by the initial age-related variance. This ratio can be interpreted as an estimate of the importance of the mediator because it indicates the proportion of the age-related variance in the measure of cognitive performance that is shared, or in common, with the mediator. In terms of Figure 1.10, the ratio is equivalent to the length of the arrow relative to the height of the column representing the effects of age alone, and to the size of the shaded region in the Venn diagrams relative to the total region of overlap between age and cognition. In order to express the results in terms of the percentage by which the age-related variance is attenuated when the index of the hypothesized mediator is controlled, the ratio can be multiplied by 100.

Decisions about degree of importance are always subjective, but it is possible to propose some tentative guidelines. For example, if the attenuation is less than 20%, then the influence can be considered small, if it is between 20% and 40% it might be considered interesting, and if it is between 40% and 60% it can be considered important. Attenuations of 60% or more are definitely major, and perhaps even critical, in the sense that any other influences involved in the age–cognition relation are either small or non-existent. This classification admittedly is arbitrary, but it is indisputable that the influence is larger, and consequently of greater potential consequence, when the percentage attenuation values are at the high end of this continuum.

METHODOLOGICAL REQUIREMENTS OF STATISTICAL CONTROL PROCEDURES

There are several desirable characteristics, or possibly even requirements, of research based on statistical control procedures. One is that the sample sizes should be fairly large. This is important because the purpose of these procedures is to obtain estimates of the magnitude of particular relations, or of the relevant proportions of variance, and the precision of both types of estimates varies directly with sample size. Moreover, large samples are especially important when, as is expected if true mediation is occurring, some of the variables have moderate to high correlations with one another such that their unique influences might be difficult to distinguish, and when the interest is in comparing proportions of variance rather than simply determining if a single variance estimate is significantly greater than zero. Research with small samples often is inadequate because the estimates of the relations and the variance proportions have wide confidence intervals, and because the values can be greatly influenced by a few extreme observations.

I tend to rely on samples of 100 or more in studies using statistical control procedures, and whenever possible, try to include adults from a wide range of ages rather than only from two extreme groups. Extreme groups can be used in these types of studies, but the resulting age relations are inflated because the variance from the middle groups is omitted. There is also a greater likelihood that adults of different ages vary on other relevant characteristics when they are recruited from different sources, as is usually the case in research involving adults from quite different age ranges.

A second desirable characteristic of research based on statistical control procedures, and indeed of all research, is reliable assessment of the relevant variables. It is particularly important in research involving statistical control procedures that a large proportion of the variance in each variable is systematic because only the systematic variance is available for association with other variables. Minimization of unsystematic variance also is important because estimates of the magnitude of relations between variables can be distorted when the variables contain unsystematic variance in the form of measurement error. It may be possible to eliminate all measurement error only by dealing with latent constructs, but an indication of the potential severity of the problem can be obtained if the reliability of the relevant measures is known. My approach has been to try to maximize reliability by aggregation of variables, and to obtain estimates of reliability whenever possible to ensure that small or no relations are not simply due to unreliable measurement.

A third characteristic that is desirable in all research, but especially in research based on statistical control procedures, is valid assessment of the theoretical constructs. Validity can be investigated by determining the pattern of relations the variable has with other variables (as in the psychometric tradition), or by determining its susceptibility to various manipulations (as in the experimental tradition). That is, two variables are likely to represent a common construct if they are highly related, or if they exhibit similar susceptibility to assorted manipulations. Procedures used to examine these characteristics are referred to as *convergent validity* and *converging operations*. On the other hand, the variables probably represent different constructs if they are unrelated to one another, or if they exhibit differential susceptibility to various manipulations. These kinds of outcomes usually are interpreted as evidence for discriminant validity or dissociation.

Both aspects of validity are critical in the context of research using statistical control procedures to investigate age–cognition relations. Convergent validity is important because if the variables used in the composites are not related to each other, or if they do not exhibit similar relations with other variables, then they may not all be measuring the intended construct. Discriminant validity is important because if the age, mediator, and cognition constructs are not distinct, then an index of the potential mediator may be simply another measure of age (e.g., the year in which one graduated from high school), or another measure of cognition (e.g., an alternative measure of the same cognitive ability). Statistical control results would be meaningless in these situations because in the former case, one index of age is removed from another index of age, and in the latter case one measure of cognition is removed from another measure of cognition.

Construct validity is a vulnerable aspect of most research, including that in which I have been involved. However, there is a very real sense in which the establishment of construct validity is as much a goal or an outcome of research as it is a prerequisite. That is, research generally starts with hypotheses about linkages between constructs, and linkages between constructs and the variables selected to represent those constructs. The outcome of the research therefore is likely to be informative both about the validity of the relations between the constructs, and about the validity of the variables as measures of the constructs. The investigation of construct validity thus can be considered an ongoing function of research because a primary purpose of research is to clarify and refine what is meant by the key theoretical constructs.

There are many potentially relevant studies that don't meet the guidelines just outlined because of small samples, and the use of single variables with little or no evidence of reliability or validity. I do not emphasize results from such studies because I believe one can have greater confidence in results derived from studies that come closer to meeting the aforementioned criteria.

SUMMARY OF STRATEGY

It is useful at this point to summarize the research strategy to be followed in attempting to investigate the mechanisms responsible for age–cognition relations. The first step is to postulate one or more potential mediators, and to identify appropriate indicators of those mediators. Data are then collected in the form of measures of the mediators and of cognition from relatively large samples of adults across a wide range of ages. Next, statistical control procedures are applied to determine the degree to which the age–cognition relations are attenuated when the level of the mediator is held constant. If the results from the initial statistical control procedures are interesting or important, then the assessment of the mediator can be refined, and the research replicated. Replication serves both to confirm the results, and to provide more precise estimates of the magnitude of the mediational influence. If the mediator continues to be important, then one can conclude that there is variance common to age, cognition, and the measure representing the hypothesized mediator. However, a result such as this does not necessarily imply that the hypothesized mediator directly contributes to the relations between age and cognition because the index measure could be a surrogate or a proxy for another construct that is not measured. Statistical control procedures also are not very informative about how or why the relation occurs. It is in these last two respects that the experimental approach is useful because once it is established that the relations do exist, analytical experimental procedures can be used to try to determine exactly how the mediation occurs. Both approaches are therefore valuable because without statistical control methods it is difficult to be certain that the variables are important in the age–cognition relation, and without experimental analysis procedures it is difficult to specify the responsible mechanisms.

TYPES OF MEDIATORS

Two major types of mediators can be distinguished according to whether the important influences are distal or proximal in nature (Salthouse, 1991b). Distal mediators are those originating at an earlier period in one's life, and whose influence often extends for a long time.

Factors such as childhood nutrition, cultural stimulation in early life, quantity and quality of education, and various kinds of experience, including those associated with one's occupation, are all examples of distal mediators.

Consider the variable of education, which is a distal influence because it usually occurs in the first 20 years of life, although its influence may continue throughout one's entire life. Because of the trend toward increased education over the past 50 years, the average older adult typically has received fewer years of education than the average young adult. Quantity of education therefore might be postulated to be a potential mediator of age–cognition relations if increased age is associated with lower levels of education, and if lower levels of education are associated with poorer performance on cognitive tests.

Educational influences often are assessed in terms of the number of years the individual reports that he or she attended school. This is a very crude measure, and in some regions of the United States it may not even be correlated highly with the highest grade successfully completed. It nevertheless can be used as an initial index of the education factor, and the amount of attenuation of age–cognition relations when it is controlled can be determined by means of multiple regression procedures. Results from analyses of this type with the same cognitive measures illustrated in Figure 1.6, expressed in terms of the percentage attenuation of the age–cognition relations, are illustrated in Figure 1.11. It is obvious that the attenuation in these variables was very weak, indicating that variation in amount of education was associated with only a small proportion of age-related variance.

Years of education is a coarse variable, and its status is ambiguous because it is not clear whether a greater amount of education is a cause or a consequence of higher levels of cognitive ability (see Salthouse, 1991b, for further discussion). Regardless of what the variable means, however, the results illustrated in Figure 1.11 suggest that amount of education is unlikely to be an important mediator of age–cognition relations.

Another possible distal determinant of age–cognition relations is the experience one has accumulated across one's life. The idea that experience mediates age–cognition relations is sometimes known as the Disuse Perspective, and is reflected in the cliche, "Use it or lose it." Because it may be unreasonable to expect effects of general

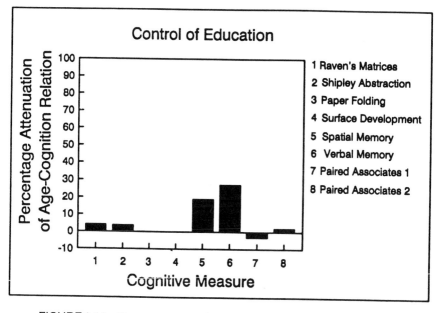

FIGURE 1.11   Percentage attenuation of age–cognition relations after statistical control of self-reported years of education. Data sets are the same as those in Figure 1.6.

experience on all aspects of cognition, experience probably is most meaningful as a potential mediator when it is conceptualized in a relatively narrow or focused manner. That is, total amount of physical, social, and mental activity may be too amorphous and undifferentiated a concept to expect large influences on particular measures of cognition. My own research therefore has concentrated on relations between specific experience (i.e., with spatial abilities) and specific measures of cognition (i.e., performance on tests of spatial ability). Amount of relevant experience usually has been estimated on the basis of self reports.

In one study, reported by Salthouse and Mitchell (1990), adults between 20 and 80 years of age performed a series of cognitive tests, including two (paper folding and surface development) assessing spatial ability. Three hundred and forty three of the participants in this project also completed a questionnaire asking about their experience with activities presumed to require spatial abilities. The questionnaire responses were analyzed with exploratory factor analysis procedures to identify a spatial experience factor, which was then treated as an index of an experience mediator and used in statistical control procedures. The R^2 associated with age in the prediction of a composite measure of spatial ability was reduced from .206 to .188 after control of this experience index. This corresponds to an attenuation of the age–cognition relations of only 8.7%.

A similar study was reported recently by Salthouse (1991c). The procedures in this study resembled those in the Salthouse and Mitchell (1990) study, but the spatial tasks were designed to be more relevant to occupational activities of mechanical engineers (i.e., they required interpreting orthographic representations of three-dimensional objects). A total of 132 adults between 21 and 80 years of age participated in the project, with many of them recruited from companies employing mechanical engineers or users of CAD/CAM systems. As in the Salthouse and Mitchell (1990) study, a relevant experience factor derived from questionnaire responses was used as the index of an experience mediator. The proportion of variance in the composite measure of spatial ability associated with age was reduced from .119 to .104 after statistical control of the experience factor. The previous results therefore were replicated by the finding of only small (i.e., 12.6%) attenuation of the age–cognition relations after control of an index of relevant experience.

Self-reports are probably not the ideal method of evaluating amount of relevant experience. The conclusion that experience only exerts a small influence on age–cognition relations is nonetheless supported by the finding in another study that similar patterns of age-related declines in spatial tasks were apparent in a sample of architects and in a sample of unselected adults (Salthouse, Babcock, Skovronek, Mitchell, & Palmon, 1990). At least based on the results of these studies, therefore, it does not appear that amount of experience is an important mediator of the relations between age and spatial measures of cognition.

It is frequently difficult to obtain complete and accurate assessments of distal influences because the relevant events may have occurred 50 to 70 years earlier. Moreover, even when the desired information is available at a group level, it often is not detailed enough to be useful in analyses at the level of individuals. As an example, estimates of the average nutritional intake or the level of cultural stimulation might be derived at different historical periods for particular geographical regions, but it is much more difficult to obtain the relevant information for specific individuals across their entire lives. It also may not merely be how much education or experience one has accumulated that is important, but how it is distributed over time, its quality, breadth, and so forth. Because detailed information at the level of individuals is needed to allow meaningful investigation of mediators with statistical control procedures, these procedures may have only limited usefulness with distal mediators.

Proximal mediators are factors operating, or at least evaluated, at the time of assessment. Examples of proximal mediators are sensory capacities, health status, and quantity or quality of knowledge. Because the relevant information usually corresponds to a characteristic of the individual that can be evaluated at the time of testing, statistical control procedures may be more feasible with proximal influences than with distal influences.

Health status is a very plausible proximal mediator of age–cognition relations because increased age often is associated with poorer health, and health status can be expected to affect level of cognitive functioning. In many research studies health is evaluated by asking the individual to assess his or her own overall health on a scale ranging from poor to excellent. Self assessments of this type are obviously a very crude means of evaluating health status, but they are not completely lacking in validity because self-ratings of health have been found to be significantly correlated with physician evaluations, number of prescription medications, and survival (see references in Salthouse, 1991b; and Salthouse, Kausler, & Saults, 1990). Results using self-reported health status as a control variable in multiple regression analyses of the influence of age on the same measures of cognitive performance represented in Figures 1.6 and 1.11 are illustrated in Figure 1.12. As was the case with the education and experience variables, these results indicate that the attenuation of the age–cognition relations is very small.

The results summarized in Figure 1.12 do not mean that health status has no effect on cognitive functioning, but merely that health status doesn't appear to be a major factor contributing to the negative relations between age and cognition in these particular samples. Undiagnosed medical problems not reflected in the self-report measures obviously could exist, but if so, they are apparently not severe enough to influence self-perceived health. Because pronounced

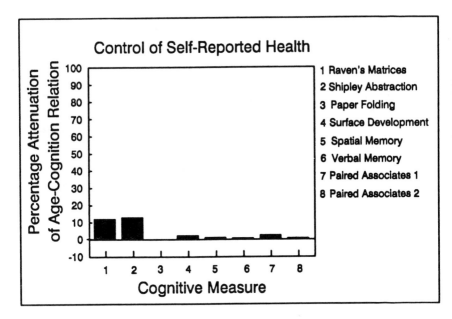

FIGURE 1.12 Percentage attenuation of age–cognition relations after statistical control of self-reported health status. Data sets are the same as those in Figure 1.6.

age relations are still evident in people who consider themselves to be healthy, these results suggest that health, at least when assessed by self-report measures, is unlikely to be an important mediator of the age–cognition relations of interest in the present context.

PROCESS-RELATED PROXIMAL MEDIATORS

Another category of proximal mediators are what might be termed *process-related proximal mediators*. These are potential mediators that are close to the outcome behavior that is to be explained. They are essentially characteristics of the individual's current processing associated with his or her observed level of performance. The major limitation of focusing on process-related mediators is that the outcome of research based on such mediators could be considered only refined description because little information is available concerning why or how the process differences originated. However, the eventual investigation of distal determinants almost certainly will be more effective when the behavioral differences to be explained have been described in the most parsimonious and integrative manner. In this respect, therefore, an interest in process-related mediators appears both justifiable and worthwhile.

The primary focus in much of my recent research has been on the role of working memory and speed of processing as proximal, process-oriented, mediators of age–cognition relations. That research is the topic of the next two chapters.

Chapter 2
Working Memory as a Potential Mediator

Working memory is the hypothesized mental work region where new and old information interact to create new products. The most salient characteristic of working memory is that it has definite limits, a fact made very apparent when one tries to perform a task containing many steps, none of which are difficult to perform in isolation. As an example, consider two variables with initial values of 7 and 3, respectively. Now perform the following operations: Subtract 2 from the first, add 1 to the second, add 3 to the first, subtract 4 from the first, and add 5 to the second. What is the current value of the first variable? This task is challenging not because any single operation is difficult, but because earlier values of the variables may be lost when new operations are performed. Errors occur because your limits for temporary storage and processing are exceeded, as though you have "run out" of working memory.

A more commonplace example of the operation of working memory occurs when you look up a telephone number, and then are interrupted to answer a quick question. The likelihood that you will still remember the telephone number is postulated to be a function, at least in part, of your working memory capabilities.

As might be inferred from these examples, working memory is a hypothetical "entity" or "process" (the vagueness is deliberate), responsible for preserving information while simultaneously processing the same or other information. It is assumed to be an essential factor in many cognitive tasks, and is considered by many researchers to be a potentially important mediator of the relations between age and cognition. In fact, something analogous to working memory has been mentioned in this connection at least since the time of Welford's (1958) classic book. (See Salthouse, 1990, for a review.)

The interest in working memory as a potential mediator of age–cognition relations is understandable because working memory limitations are plausible sources of impairments in both the quantity and quality of performance. That is, quantitative aspects of performance can be affected when working memory is limited because the rate of solving cognitive tasks may be reduced if more time-consuming exchanges of information to and from stable long-term memory systems are required. Limitations of working memory also might affect quality of performance if the solution to a task requires a greater amount of simultaneously available information than that which can be maintained within the constraints of an ineffective working memory system.

Working memory does not correspond to the number of slots or to a fixed storage space as in earlier conceptions of short-term memory, but instead it refers to the flexible allocation of both storage and processing. Perhaps the best metaphor of working memory at the current time is Broadbent's (1971) characterization of working memory as like the surface of a desk. That is, working memory is postulated to be similar to a desktop in that it can be used both to store materials, and to work on those, or other, materials. The desktop metaphor also is consistent with the possibility of a tradeoff between storage and processing, which is a prominent characteristic of recent views of working memory.

MEASUREMENT OF WORKING MEMORY

Two methods can be used to assess working memory when it is defined in terms of concurrent storage and processing. One method, which was first used by Baddeley and Hitch (1974), involves measuring the efficiency of processing with concurrent storage. Working memory functioning in this method usually is assessed in units of efficiency or time. The second method expresses working memory in units of number of items remembered or span, and consists of measuring the capacity of storage with concurrent processing. Daneman and Carpenter (1980) were among the first to use this method of assessing working memory.

In my research I have relied on two measures of the latter type. The primary tasks used to obtain these measures, the computation span task and the listening span task, are illustrated in Figure 2.1. It can be

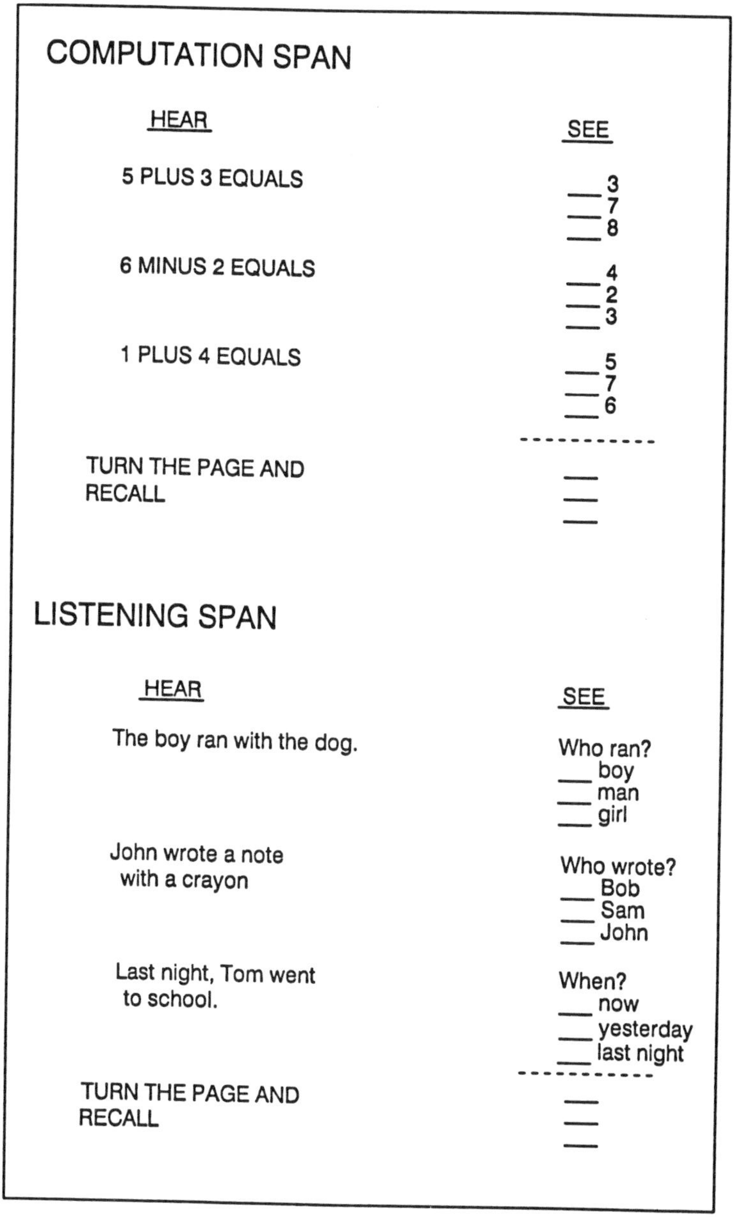

COMPUTATION SPAN

<u>HEAR</u>

<u>SEE</u>

5 PLUS 3 EQUALS

___ 3
___ 7
___ 8

6 MINUS 2 EQUALS

___ 4
___ 2
___ 3

1 PLUS 4 EQUALS

___ 5
___ 7
___ 6

- - - - - - - - - - -

TURN THE PAGE AND
RECALL

___

___

LISTENING SPAN

<u>HEAR</u>

<u>SEE</u>

The boy ran with the dog.

Who ran?
___ boy
___ man
___ girl

John wrote a note
with a crayon

Who wrote?
___ Bob
___ Sam
___ John

Last night, Tom went
to school.

When?
___ now
___ yesterday
___ last night

- - - - - - - - - - -

TURN THE PAGE AND
RECALL

___

___

FIGURE 2.1   Illustration of events in typical trials in the computation span
and listening span tasks.

seen that both processing and preservation of information are required in each task. That is, the examinee must answer arithmetic problems and remember the last digit in the problems, or must answer sentence comprehension questions and remember the last word in the sentences. Performance in each task is evaluated in terms of the number of items remembered when the required processing was also performed correctly. A typical procedure involves presenting three trials each with from one to seven arithmetic problems or sentences, and then defining the span as the largest number of items with correct responses on both the storage and processing aspects in at least two of the three trials.

Correlations between the computation span measure and other measures presumed to reflect working memory are mostly between .4 and .6 in samples with restricted age ranges. As an example, in a study published in 1988 (Salthouse, 1988b), young and old adults were administered four memory span tasks including computation span, backwards digit span, a missing-digit span, and a subtract-two span task in which the number two had to be subtracted from each digit. The median correlation among these measures was .44 for the sample of young adults, and .45 for the sample of older adults. A study reported by Babcock and Salthouse (1990) used a spatial line span task in which research participants attempted to remember the positions of lines while also creating other lines by connecting specified dots. The correlation between this spatial line span and the computation span in a sample of young adults was .40.

Despite a reasonable range of material (i.e., words, digits, and line positions), processing requirements (i.e., arithmetic, sentence comprehension, and line creation), and presentation modalities (i.e., auditory and visual), most of the correlations among the measures hypothesized to reflect working memory have been in the moderate range. Furthermore, because the reliabilities of the measures were far from perfect, and usually between .6 and .8, the correlations undoubtedly would have been even higher if corrections for unreliability had been employed. Results such as these therefore suggest that working memory is a meaningful construct that can be assessed with several different kinds of tasks.

Age relations in the computation span and listening span tasks, with about 200 adults represented in each decade, are illustrated in Figure 2.2. The correlations with age in this sample of 1,270 adults were –.41

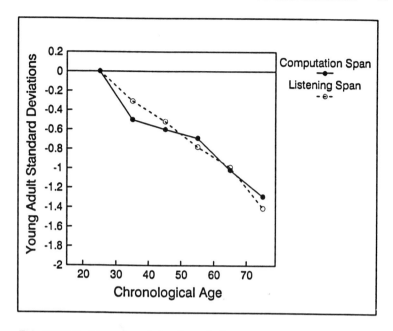

FIGURE 2.2   Means at each decade, scaled in young adult standard deviation units, for the computation span and listening span measures. Data from Salthouse (1991a) and Salthouse and Babcock (1991) and some unpublished data.

for the computation span measure and –.45 for the listening span measure. The correlation between the two measures was .60, which suggests that only 36% of the variance in each measure was common to the other measure. However, the most interesting question from the current perspective is not the proportion of the total variance that the variables have in common, but rather the proportion of the age-related variance in each variable that is shared with the other variable. Estimates of these latter values can be obtained by means of statistical control techniques, with the logic of these procedures illustrated in Figure 2.3.

Notice that the overlap of two variables can be evaluated either with respect to the total variance in a variable, or with respect to the variance in the variable that is also common to age. In order to determine the degree to which the variables share age-related variance, multiple regression procedures can be used to determine the proportion of age-related variance in each variable before and after statistical control

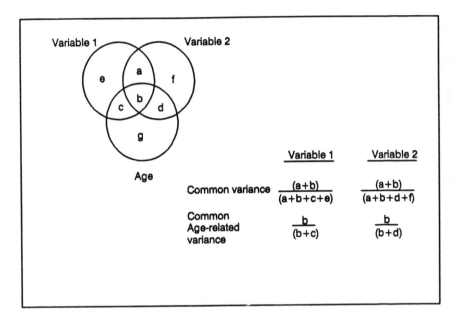

FIGURE 2.3 Schematic representation of the partitioning of the total variance, or of the age-related variance, into regions shared and not shared with another variable.

of the other variable. The difference between the initial and the residual variance divided by the initial variance indicates the amount of attenuation of the initial age-related variance, which in this context can be interpreted as an estimate of the age-related variance in one variable that is common with the age-related variance in another variable.

The R^2 associated with age in the regression equation predicting the variance in the computation span measure was .164, but the age-associated variance was reduced to .023 when age was entered in the regression equation after the listening span measure. This corresponds to an attenuation, or percentage of shared age-related variance, of 86.0%. The R^2 for age in the prediction of the listening span measure was .202, which was reduced to .050 after variance in the computation span measure was controlled. In this case the attenuation, and thus the percentage of common variance, was 75.2%. These results therefore indicate that the computation span and listening span measures are very similar with respect to age-related influences because an average of about 80% of the age-related variance in one measure is shared with the other measure.

The computation span and listening span tasks also have been implemented on a computer to allow self-paced presentation of the stimulus material. The computer-administered tasks involved the same arithmetic problems and sentences, but the rate at which the items were presented was completely under the control of the examinee, and the sequence of trials was terminated when the individual was correct on less than two of the three trials with a given number of items. A total of 280 adults from a wide range of ages have performed the computer-administered versions of these working memory tasks (Salthouse, in press-a). The results were very similar to those with the original versions of the tasks as the age correlations were −.45 for the computation span measure and −.39 for the listening span measure, and the correlation between the two measures was .53. The percentages of age-related variance common to the two measures, as estimated from statistical control procedures, were 81% and 66%.

The results just described suggest that the computation span and listening span measures have several desirable characteristics as indexes of the hypothesized working memory mediator. First, they have face validity in the sense that both tasks possess the defining characteristics of working memory in requiring both processing and storage. Second, the measures have been found to be correlated negatively with age, as expected if they reflect a mediator contributing to the negative relations between age and cognition. And third, the measures are correlated moderately with each other, and have a considerable degree of overlap in the amount of age-related variance. These kinds of measures therefore have been used as indexes of the hypothesized working memory mediator in statistical control procedures in five recent studies.

STATISTICAL CONTROL RESULTS

An initial study, published in 1988 (Salthouse, 1988b), used backwards digit span as the working memory measure, and the average of time and accuracy in four cognitive tasks (i.e., paper folding, mental synthesis, and two geometric analogies tests) as the composite cognitive measure. (Decision time was reflected so that higher scores corresponded to better performance.) Participants in this study consisted of 100 young adults and 100 older adults. Multiple regression procedures on the composite cognition measure revealed that age was associated with an R^2 of .428 when it was the only predictor of cognitive performance, but this was reduced to .309 after statistical control of the backwards digit span measure of working memory. This attenuation of 27.8% is not very impressive, but it is larger than that evident with control of either amount of education (Figure 1.11) or self-reported health (Figure 1.12), and the backwards digit span task may not have provided the optimal assessment of working memory.

A study published in 1989 used the computation span task to measure working memory, with the average accuracy in two cognitive tasks, paper folding and integrative reasoning, serving as the composite cognitive measure (Salthouse, Mitchell, Skovronek, & Babcock, 1989). A total of 120 adults, 20 in each decade from the 20s through the 70s, participated in this project. The R^2 for age when it was the only predictor of cognitive performance was .346, but this was reduced to .172, an attenuation of 50.3%, when the age effects were examined after controlling for the variance in the computation span measure.

The most recent studies examining the mediational influence of working memory on age–cognition relations were reported in an article published in 1991 (Salthouse, 1991a). Each of these studies involved over 220 adults ranging from 18 to 83 years of age who performed the computation span and listening span tasks in addition to several cognitive tests. The cognitive tests performed by participants in Study 1 were the Raven's Advanced Progressive Matrices Test and the Shipley Abstraction Test, while those in Studies 2 and 3 involved paper folding, integrative reasoning, geometric analogies, and cube assembly. The R^2 values associated with age in each study when age was the only predictor of the composite cognitive performance measure were .305, .169, and .255 in Studies 1, 2, and 3, respectively. The percentages by which these values were reduced after controlling the influence of the composite working memory measure were 87.9% for Study 1, 55.0% for Study 2, and 52.5% for Study 3.

The results from these five studies, expressed in terms of the percentage attenuation of the age–cognition relations, are summarized in Figure 2.4. The overall pattern suggests that working memory is associated with about 50% of the age-related variance in measures of

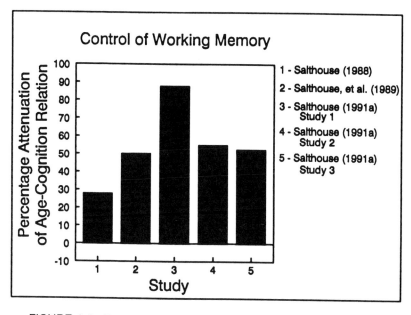

FIGURE 2.4   Percentage attenuation of the age–cognition relations after statistical control of working memory.

cognitive functioning. According to the guidelines proposed in chapter 1, working memory thus can be inferred to be an important mediator of at least some of the adult age differences in cognitive functioning.

Working memory may have even greater importance as a mediator of age–cognition relations when the cognitive measures represent power more than speed. This is apparent in analyses of measures of the percentage of attempted items answered correctly in the three studies reported in Salthouse (1991a). These measures are at least conceptually independent of the number of items attempted because they reflect how successful the individual was on the problems on which he or she worked, rather than the speed of either attempting or solving the problems. The percentages by which the age-related variance were reduced in measures of percent correct solutions after statistical control of the composite working memory measure were 98.1% for Study 1, 86.6% for Study 2, and 77.2% for Study 3.

In light of the evidence from the statistical control procedures that there are significant relations between age and working memory and between working memory and cognition, it was considered appropriate to pursue research with the second method in the investigative strategy. Analytical experimental procedures therefore were used to verify the conclusions regarding the influence of working memory on age–cognition relations, and to investigate the nature of the mechanisms that might be responsible for that influence.

MANIPULATION OF WORKING MEMORY DEMANDS

One method of investigating the influence of working memory consists of manipulating the working memory requirements of the task. The rationale underlying this manipulation is that the age differences are expected to be larger when the working memory requirements are increased because the consequences of greater demands placed on an ineffective working memory system should be more pronounced than those resulting from the same demands placed on an effective working memory system. Several cognitive tasks were therefore designed in which items within the task varied with respect to the number of required processing operations. The primary assumption was that items with a larger number of processing operations will have the greatest requirements for mental computation and bookkeeping, even if only because a greater number of, or more complex, products of earlier operations have to be maintained during the execution of subsequent operations. It thus was hypothesized that items requiring more operations would come closer to exceeding the capacities of older individuals who are postulated to have limited working memory systems, whereas smaller effects of item variation were expected among younger individuals, whose working memory systems were assumed to be more effective.

These predictions have been examined in the cube comparison test illustrated in the top panel of Figure 2.5. It can be seen that the materials for an item in this test consist of a pair of cubes, each with three visible faces containing letters in different orientations. The task for the research participant is to decide whether the two cubes could be identical, given the restriction that each face of a given cube contains a different letter. Trials within the task varied with respect to the number of 90° rotations between the two cubes.

One possible strategy for performing this task is as follows. First, determine if all of the letters on each cube face match. If not, then try

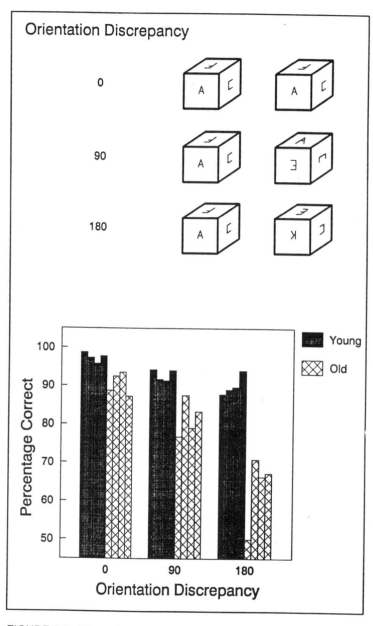

FIGURE 2.5   Illustration of cube comparison trials hypothesized to vary in working memory demands (top panel), and mean performance of young and old adults with each trial type (bottom panel).

to find a corresponding letter on the right cube and determine the number and type of rotations needed for that letter to match in orientation in the two cubes. Next, carry out the appropriate mental rotation on the other cube faces, and compare the identity and orientation of the transformed letters in the two cubes. Finally, make a decision based on the outcome of the three relevant comparisons across the two cubes. Other strategies are clearly possible, but in all cases it seems important to preserve the identity and the orientation of the letters on the cube faces after the cubes have been rotated in order to determine the correspondence between the transformed cube and the comparison or reference cube. Furthermore, both the amount of information to be preserved and the amount of processing to be performed, which jointly determine the working memory requirements, increase in direct proportion to the orientation discrepancy between the two cubes.

Because the task was administered on a computer, both decision time and decision accuracy were measured. However, only the decision accuracy results are of interest here because the research participants were encouraged to emphasize accuracy rather than speed. The results on this task from four independent studies (Salthouse & Skovronek, in press), with from 24 to 50 adults in each age group, are displayed in the bottom of Figure 2.5. Notice that, as expected, the drop in accuracy for older adults was greater than that for young adults in all four studies. This pattern was confirmed by the presence of statistically significant Age × Orientation Discrepancy interactions in each study.

A project reported in 1988 involved 100 young adults and 100 older adults who each performed several cognitive tasks at four levels of complexity, or hypothesized working memory demands (Salthouse, 1988b). Both time and accuracy were emphasized, and therefore composite performance indexes were created by combining the time and accuracy values in a given task. This was accomplished by determining the z-scores based on the distribution of scores across both age groups and all trial types, and then averaging the z-scores for accuracy and time (with the latter reflected so that higher scores represented better performance).

One of the tasks performed by the participants in the 1988 project was the geometric analogies task illustrated in the top panel of Figure 2.6. Notice that the stimulus materials for a trial consisted of four

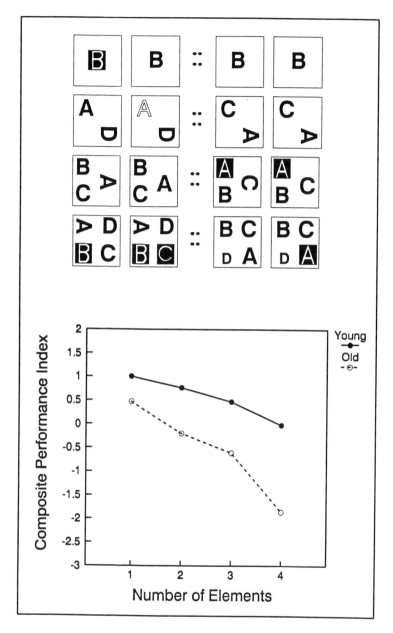

FIGURE 2.6   Illustration of geometric analogies trials hypothesized to vary in working memory demands (top panel), and mean performance of young and old adults with each trial type (bottom panel).

boxes, each containing one to four letters varying in orientation, size, font, and background. The task was to decide whether the relations between the elements in the first and second terms (boxes) were identical to those between the elements in the third and fourth terms (i.e., does the third term have the same relation to the fourth term as the first term has to the second term?). Trials within the task varied with respect to the number of elements per term because of the assumption that working memory demands would be greater when more variables had to be monitored during the solution process. As can be seen in the bottom panel of Figure 2.6, the effects of these manipulations were larger in older adults than in young adults.

A second task performed by the participants in this project was a mental synthesis task in which pattern fragments had to be integrated into a unitary composite, and then compared with a target pattern. Stimuli in this task, examples of which are illustrated in the top panel of Figure 2.7, consisted of a pattern composed of 12 line segments on the right of an equal sign, and one to four boxes each containing either 12, 6, 4, or 3 line segment fragments on the left of the equal sign. The number of frames containing pattern segments varied across trials because it was assumed that the greater requirements of processing (integration operations), and/or storage (number of pattern frag-ments), associated with more frames would lead to larger demands on working memory. The results with this task, illustrated in the bottom panel of Figure 2.7, confirmed the expectation that the consequences of the number-of-frames manipulation would be greater in older adults than in young adults.

The Age × Complexity (i.e., number of elements per term or number of frames) interactions were statistically significant in both the analogies and synthesis tasks, and very similar patterns in both tasks were obtained in an independent replication study in the same project. The functions in Figures 2.6 and 2.7 were nearly linear, and thus regression equations relating the composite performance index to task demand were computed for the individual research participants in each task. The slopes of these equations are of particular interest because they indicate the amount of decrease in the composite performance index with each increment in task demand (i.e., additional elements per term in the analogies task, and additional to-be-integrated frames in the synthesis task). Correlations between age and the slope parameters were $-.56$ in the analogies task, and $-.33$ in the synthesis

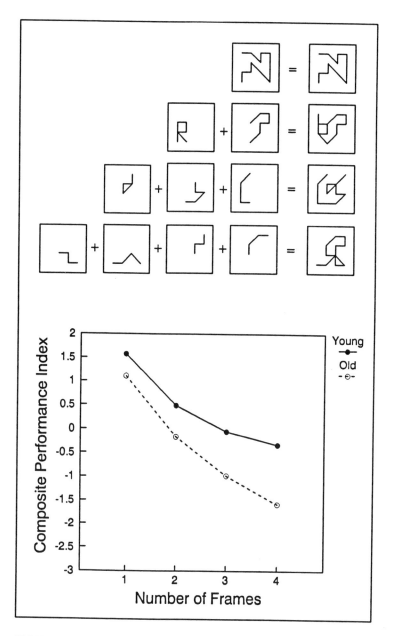

FIGURE 2.7   Illustration of mental synthesis trials hypothesized to vary in working memory demands (top panel), and mean performance of young and old adults with each trial type (bottom panel).

task. Both values were significantly greater than zero, and because they indicate a greater performance decline with older age, they are consistent with the significant Age × Complexity interactions also found in these data.

Another intriguing result in this project was the finding that the complexity slopes from the two tasks were correlated significantly with each other, that is, $r = .46$ (and $r = .33$ after partialing age). In other words, the amount by which performance declined with increases in the number of elements per term in the analogies task was related to the amount by which performance declined with increases in the number of frames in the synthesis task. This finding provides additional support for the hypothesis that a common working memory factor was involved in the across-trial variation in both tasks.

The results from the three tasks just described are in agreement with those from the statistical control procedures because, like the earlier results, they imply the existence of at least two factors contributing to the age differences in cognition. One factor is the working memory influence presumed to be responsible for the increase in the magnitude of the age differences with greater demands on working memory. The nature of the other factor is unspecified, but it can be inferred to correspond to whatever is responsible for the age differences in the simplest conditions in which there are relatively few working memory demands.

The influence of the latter determinants might be minimized by eliminating the data from research participants who have low levels of performance in the simplest conditions in the task. Performance of these individuals may be poor because of comprehension difficulties, sensorimotor problems, low motivation, or various other reasons, but whatever the cause, the effects of influences that vary across trials, such as working memory demands, could be obscured if the data from such individuals were included in the analyses.

The strategy of restricting the analyses to data from research participants who perform above a specified criterion in the simplest condition in the task was adopted in a study published in 1989 (Salthouse, Mitchell, Skovronek, & Babcock, 1989). A total of 120 adults between 20 and 79 years of age participated in this study. Each individual performed computer-administered paper folding and integrative reasoning tasks that allowed self-paced presentation of the materials and automatic monitoring of both study time and decision time. Although decision time was measured, accuracy of the decisions was emphasized much more than speed, and consequently the results are discussed in terms of the accuracy measures. For the analyses reported below, only the data from the research participants with accuracy of at least 85% in the simplest conditions in the tasks were included.

Examples of trials in the paper folding task are illustrated in the top panel of Figure 2.8. Note that each trial consisted of a display of rectangles representing a piece of paper being folded, and a hole punched through the folded paper. The goal was to determine whether the pattern of holes on the right of the equal sign would result from the displayed sequence of folds and punch location. The task is very similar to the paper-and-pencil paper-folding test illustrated in Figure 1.2, but because it was implemented on a computer, the folds were presented sequentially and in a dynamic rather than static format. Working memory demands were manipulated by increasing the number of folds presented prior to the simulated hole punch because more information had to be remembered and coordinated as more folds were presented. As can be seen in the bottom of Figure 2.8, the accuracy declines were larger at older ages. Because the accuracy decreases were nearly linear, the effects could be represented in terms of the slope of the function relating accuracy to the number of folds. The correlation between age and this slope was −.47.

Examples of trials in the integrative reasoning task are illustrated in the top panel of Figure 2.9. It can be seen that a trial consisted of a series of premises describing the relation between pairs of variables, followed by a question about the relation between two variables. The task was to answer the question about the effect of a specified change of one variable on another variable on the basis of the stated relations between those and other variables. Working memory demands were manipulated by means of the number of premises presented prior to the question because more information must be preserved and either integrated or coordinated when trials contain more premises. Results from this task, illustrated in the bottom panel of Figure 2.9, were similar to those with the paper-folding task because the accuracy declines were steeper at older ages. The correlation between age and the slope of the regression equation relating decision accuracy to number of presented premises was −.46.

As in the earlier study, a correlation also was computed between

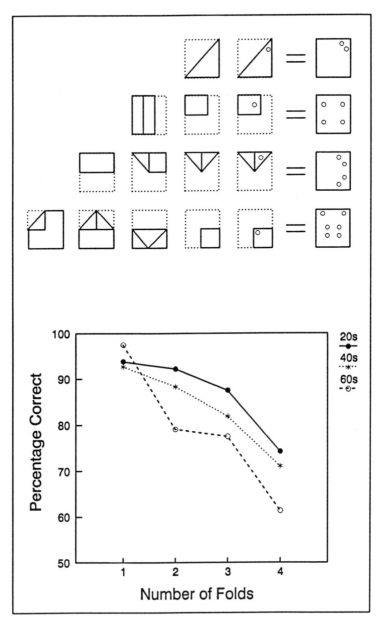

FIGURE 2.8   Illustration of paper folding trials hypothesized to vary in working memory demands (top panel), and mean performance of adults in their 20s, 40s, and 60s with each trial type (bottom panel).

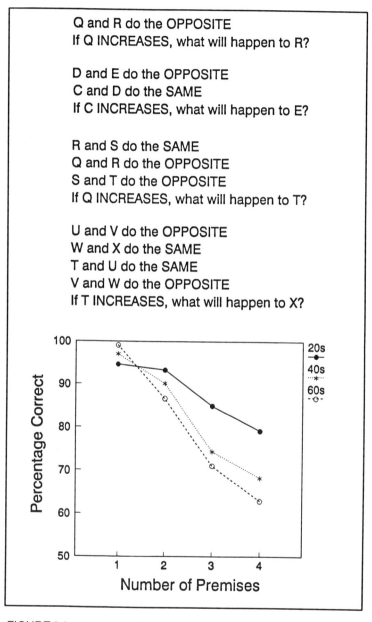

FIGURE 2.9   Illustration of integrative reasoning trials hypothesized to vary in working memory demands (top panel), and mean performance of adults in their 20s, 40s, and 60s with each trial type (bottom panel).

the slopes relating cognitive performance to task complexity (i.e., number of folds in the paper folding task, and number of premises in the integrative reasoning task). The correlation of $r = .63$ (and $r = .54$ after partialing age), was significantly greater than zero, and it actually was greater than 1.0 after employing a correction for attenuation due to measurement unreliability. This result indicates that a large proportion of the variance in the slope measures, and perhaps even all of the reliable variance, was shared or common variance.

The results from these studies manipulating working memory demands by varying the number of required operations appear to provide strong support for the role of working memory as a mediator of the age differences in at least some cognitive tasks. Not only does the magnitude of the age differences increase with increases in hypothesized working memory demands in at least five different cognitive tasks, but the magnitude of the performance differences in one task has been found to be significantly correlated with that in another task. This latter result, which was confirmed in two independent studies involving four different cognitive tasks, provides converging evidence that a common factor is involved in the susceptibility to increased working memory demands across tasks with quite distinct materials and operations.

However, not all variations in accuracy can be attributed to changes in the influence of working memory. As an example, I recently have found that there are substantial differences in item difficulty (mean accuracy in individual items) in matrix reasoning tasks, but that there are no systematic differences across the items in the magnitude of the relations with either age or working memory (Salthouse, under review). This pattern of significant variation in accuracy across items, but constant influences of age and working memory, appears to be reliable because it was evident in three independent studies with different methods and materials.

It should be pointed out that although the results just described do not provide support for the working memory mediation hypothesis, they are not necessarily inconsistent with that hypothesis. That is, the results would contradict the postulated linkage between age and working memory only if the working memory influence increased with item difficulty (implicating working memory as a factor in the accuracy variation), but there was no change in the magnitude of the age influence (indicating that working memory involvement was not sufficient to produce age differences). Instead, the results of these studies indicate that neither age nor working memory seems to be involved in the across-item accuracy variations.

STATISTICAL CONTROL ANALYSES OF SIMPLE AND COMPLEX COGNITIVE TASKS

The results described above are consistent in indicating that the age differences in many cognitive tasks become greater as the tasks are made more complex in the sense of requiring more processing operations that can be presumed to increase demands on working memory. Another means of examining the role of working memory as a factor contributing to larger age differences in complex versions of cognitive tasks involves the use of statistical control procedures. Two types of analyses are relevant in this connection. One focuses on the question of how much of the *total variance* in measures of performance in complex versions of a task is associated with measures of working memory. The second analysis is concerned with the question of how much of the *age-related variance* in measures of performance in complex versions of a task is associated with measures of working memory. In both cases the interest is in determining the influence of working memory on performance in a complex version of the task after all determinants of performance in simpler versions of the task have been statistically controlled.

Data in which these types of analyses can be conducted are those from Studies 2 and 3 of Salthouse (1991a), which have been analyzed in terms of task complexity in Salthouse (in press-c). Each study involved four different cognitive tasks—integrative reasoning, geometric analogies, paper folding, and cube assembly—at three levels of task complexity (i.e., number of required operations). Average correlations between age and the percentage of correct solutions were –.060 for versions of the task with one required operation, –.240 for versions with two required operations, and –.242 for versions with three required operations. Because the greatest increase in the age relations was from one to two operations, the present analyses focus on those two versions of the tasks, which are referred to as *simple* and *complex,* respectively.

The initial analysis consisted of entering performance in the simple version of the task, along with the composite measure of working memory (computation span and listening span), as predictors of performance in the complex version of the task. Because the predictors were considered simultaneously, any influence of working memory in this analysis is independent of the factors contributing to performance in the simple version of the task. That is, any number of factors can influence performance in the simple version of the task, and all of these influences are represented, at least indirectly, when simple performance is considered as a predictor of complex performance. A significant effect of working memory on complex performance therefore would indicate that working memory exerts an influence on complex performance above and beyond any effects it might have on simple performance. The working memory influence was statistically significant in five of the eight cognitive tasks, and across all tasks it was responsible for an average of 4.01% of the total variance in performance. These results therefore imply that working memory makes a contribution to performance in complex cognitive tasks in addition to whatever contribution it makes to performance in simpler versions of the same tasks.

The second type of analysis conducted on these data is related to commonality analysis (Pedhazur, 1982), and involves evaluating the influence of two simultaneous mediators. A Venn diagram representing the overlapping regions of variance associated with two mediators affecting the relations between age and cognition is illustrated in Figure 2.10. The goal of these analyses is to estimate both the unique (i.e., regions b and c) and the common (i.e., region d) contributions of the two mediators to the age-related variance in cognition. For the current purposes the measure of performance in the complex version of the task can be considered to represent cognition, and performance in the simple version of the task and the composite measure of working memory can be considered as potential mediators. Estimates of the proportion of variance in each of the regions represented in Figure 2.10 were determined for each of the eight tasks (four tasks in each of two studies), and then these estimates were converted into percentages of age-related variance by dividing the values by the total age-related variance (i.e., a + b + c + d). These percentages, along with the average across the eight tasks, are summarized in Figure 2.11.

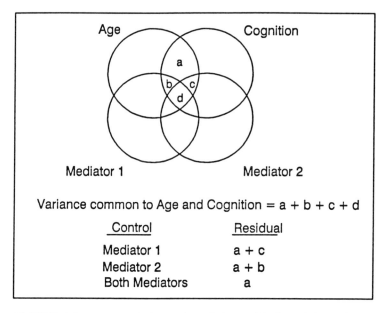

FIGURE 2.10   Schematic illustration of the partitioning of the variance among age, cognition, and two simultaneous mediators. The bottom of the figure indicates the variance regions remaining after one or both mediators have been statistically controlled.

One of the most important points to note about the results in Figure 2.11 is that, on the average, nearly 65% of the age-related variance in measures of performance in complex versions of these cognitive tasks is associated with working memory. In other words, variations in working memory appear to be responsible for the majority of the age-related variance in the performance of complex cognitive tasks, independent of the influence of age, working memory, and all other factors that contribute to performance of simpler versions of the same cognitive tasks. When considered together, therefore, the results of the two analyses just described suggest that a major reason why age differences are more pronounced in more complex cognitive tasks is because there is a greater influence of working memory in more complex tasks.

INFORMATION AVAILABILITY

Another series of experimental or analytical investigations was based on the assumption that working memory influences cognitive perfor-

TASK	STUDY	Unexplained (a)	Unique to Simple Cognition (b)	Unique to Working Memory (c)	Common to Simple Cognition and Working Memory (d)
Integrative Reasoning	1	1.5	0	94.7	3.8
	2	58.4	1.9	39.7	0
Geometric Analogies	1	11.5	0	83.2	5.3
	2	7.8	4.1	62.4	25.7
Paper Folding	1	29.8	2.3	63.8	4.1
	2	34.1	0	59.2	6.7
Cube Assembly	1	34.7	1.6	64.2	0
	2	19.0	5.0	52.3	23.7
AVERAGE		24.5	1.9	64.9	8.7

FIGURE 2.11 Percentages of unique and common contributions to the performance in complex versions of a cognitive task associated with working memory and performance in simple versions of the same cognitive task.

mance because it is responsible for maintaining information during processing. That is, impairments in working memory may lead to less information being available when it is needed during the solution of the task. Several recent studies have examined the implication that a consequence of a limitation in working memory is decreased availability of information during processing.

One project in which information availability was investigated was the Salthouse et al. (1989) study described earlier in which 120 adults between 20 and 79 years of age performed both a paper folding task and an integrative reasoning task. The method used to investigate information availability in these tasks was based on a distinction between one-relevant and all-relevant trials. Examples of the two trial types are presented in Figure 2.12. Careful inspection reveals that only the second premise (or the second fold) is relevant in the trials portrayed in the top of the figure because the question (or position of the hole punch) refers only to information presented (or manipulated) in that premise (or fold). In contrast, all of the premises (or folds) are

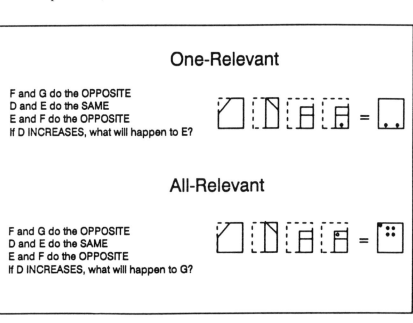

FIGURE 2.12   Illustration of distinction between integrative reasoning and paper folding trials with only one relevant premise or fold (top), and trials in which all of the premises or folds are relevant (bottom) to the decision.

relevant in the trials portrayed in the bottom panel because all of the presented information must be used to solve those problems.

The distinction between one-relevant and all-relevant trials was postulated to be useful in attempting to separate availability of information from other factors affecting decision accuracy, such as integration or coordination of information. The rationale is as follows. No integration across premises or across folds is needed if the relevant information is presented in a single premise or fold. The only requirement for an accurate decision is that the premise information be remembered and converted from the Same/Opposite format to the Increase/Decrease format in the reasoning task, and that the fold and hole information be remembered and the paper be mentally unfolded in the paper folding task. However, when more than one premise or fold is relevant, not only does the information have to be remembered and converted, but the information from several premises or folds must also be integrated or coordinated across two or more premises or folds. Comparison of the age trends in one-relevant and all-relevant trials therefore can be expected to be informative about the relative importance on decision accuracy of information availability and information integration or coordination. Because it is impossible for the research participant to determine which information is relevant until it has all been presented, decision accuracy in the one-relevant trials provides an estimate of the availability of all the information. Accuracy in all-relevant trials can be postulated to reflect the availability of the information plus the effectiveness of integration and coordination processes.

Figure 2.13 illustrates average accuracy and average decision time across two, three, and four premises or folds for one-relevant and all-relevant trials at successive decades. Trials with a single premise or fold are not included in these data because the distinction between one-relevant and all-relevant trials is not meaningful when there is only one fold or one premise. The results in the top panels of Figure 2.13 indicate that average accuracy decreased with increased age, and that the averages were virtually identical for one-relevant trials and for all-relevant trials. The nearly complete absence of a difference between the two types of trials is surprising because it suggests that the important determinant of decision accuracy in all age groups is the availability of the information, and that there is no problem at any age in integrating or coordinating information.

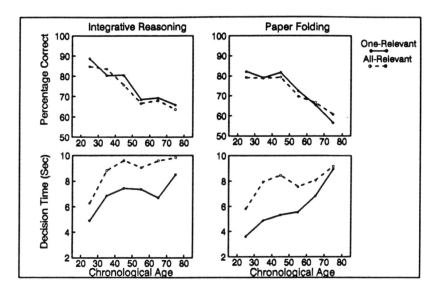

FIGURE 2.13   Decision accuracy (top), and decision time (bottom), as a function of age decade for one-relevant and all-relevant trials in the integrative reasoning and paper folding tasks.

It might be argued that there was no difference between the one-relevant trials and the all-relevant trials because this distinction was not meaningful in these tasks, perhaps because the same type of processing was carried out on all trials. Although this interpretation is plausible, it cannot be the entire explanation because the results in the bottom panels of Figure 2.13 indicate that there was a large difference in median decision time across one-relevant and all-relevant trials. When considered in combination, therefore, the decision accuracy and decision time results imply that integration or coordination processes require time during the decision phase, but if the relevant information is available, then these time-consuming operations have little or no effect on decision accuracy. In at least these two quite different tasks, a critical factor contributing to the existence and magnitude of age differences in cognitive performance appears to be the availability of relevant information while the individual is engaged in the solution of the task.

One limitation of the results just described is that the inferences about information availability were based on performance in a task that not only required preservation of the information, but conversion or transformation from one format (e.g., two variables do the SAME) to another format (e.g., what will happen if one variable is IN-CREASED?). It therefore seemed desirable to obtain a more direct measure of information availability without the need to transform information. The assumption underlying these new procedures was that it might be possible to assess information availability by interrupting some trials during the performance of the task to determine whether the earlier presented information can be accurately recognized.

One task in which this recognition probe procedure was used is the matrix reasoning task illustrated in the top of Figure 2.14. This task is based on the Raven's Advanced Progressive Matrices Test, but it involves different stimuli, and is administered on a computer instead of with paper-and-pencil procedures. The research participant still attempts to select the pattern that provides the best completion of the matrix, but the matrix and the answer-alternative displays were presented sequentially rather than simultaneously. That is, the matrix could be viewed as long as desired, and then a key was pressed to inspect the answer alternatives. Two thirds of the trials consisted of the standard sequence of the matrix followed by the answer alternatives, but on one third of the trials a recognition probe was presented instead of the answer alternatives. On these trials the participant was instructed to make a same/different decision according to whether the contents of the displayed cell had been presented earlier in that matrix position. Results of this study (Salthouse, under review), in terms of the percentage of correct responses in the matrix decisions and in the probe recognition decisions, are illustrated in the bottom panel of Figure 2.14. It is apparent that young adults were more accurate than older adults in both matrix decisions and probe recognition decisions.

A possible concern in this study is that performance in the probe task may not provide an accurate reflection of the preservation of information during processing because the individual indicated when he or she was ready to inspect the answer alternatives (or the recognition probe). It thus is conceivable that working memory may have been cleared of relevant stimulus information before the recognition probe was presented. In order to investigate this possibility, another study was conducted with a successive presentation version of the task in which the research participant examined the contents of each cell sequentially by pressing a key corresponding to the relevant cell. Although one might imagine that different processes could have been

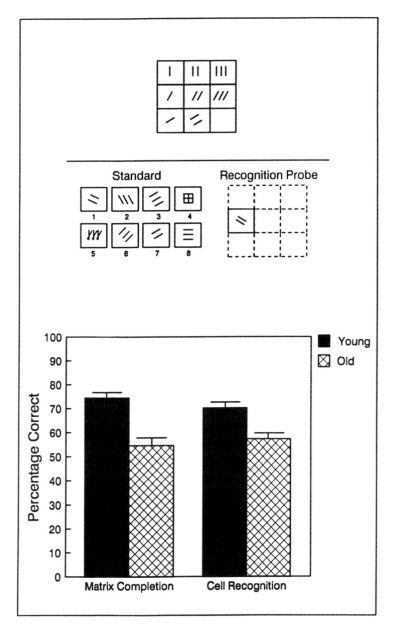

FIGURE 2.14   Illustration of successive displays in standard and recognition probe matrix reasoning trials (top), and mean accuracy (with standard errors) on both types of trials for young and old adults (bottom).

involved in the simultaneous and sequential versions of the task, this was apparently not the case because the correlation between the accuracy measures in the two versions was .73.

Because the cell contents were examined sequentially, the ongoing processing could be interrupted by occasionally probing for the recognition of the contents of a previously examined cell instead of displaying the contents of the requested cell. The results with this version of the matrix task were very similar to those with simultaneous presentation of the matrix cells in that young adults were more accurate than older adults at both matrix decisions and probe recognition decisions.

Unfortunately, other results with the probe recognition procedure have been less consistent. As an example, the procedure has been used in a successive version of the mental synthesis task by occasionally presenting probes of line segments from a previously presented frame (Salthouse, Mitchell, & Palmon, 1989). Although young adults were more accurate than older adults in the synthesis decisions, the age differences in probe recognition accuracy were statistically significant only when data were excluded from research participants with low levels of accuracy in the synthesis task. Because the same pattern was found in a second experiment, this phenomenon is apparently reliable. It is possible that low-performing individuals frequently failed to encode all of the information, and consequently age differences in information availability may have been obscured because some of the research participants might not have accurately registered the information.

The probe recognition procedure also has been used in the integrative reasoning task by presenting the premises and questions sequentially rather than simultaneously, and on a randomly selected one third of the trials presenting a recognition probe instead of a question (Salthouse, in press-d). Examples of the two types of trials are illustrated in the top panel in Figure 2.15. The bottom panel in this figure illustrates that age differences in favor of young adults were evident in both reasoning accuracy and probe recognition accuracy. However, additional analyses revealed that the probe recognition differences were reduced when data were excluded from research participants with low levels of accuracy in the reasoning decisions. Note that this is the opposite of the pattern obtained in the synthesis task, because in this case it appears that there may be no age differences in measures of recognition accuracy among the better-performing members of each age group.

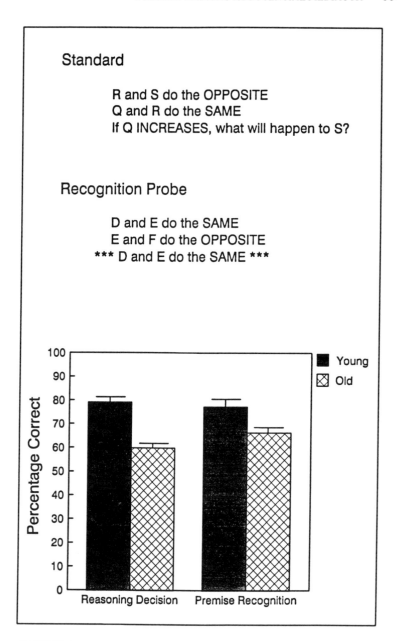

FIGURE 2.15   Illustration of successive displays in standard and recognition probe integrative reasoning trials (top), and mean accuracy (with standard errors) on both types of trials for young and old adults (bottom).

Finally, no significant age differences in probe recognition accuracy were found when the probe recognition procedure was used in a cube comparison task (Salthouse & Skovronek, in press). A sequential version of the task was administered in which the research participant pressed a key to examine each cube face, and on randomly selected trials a probe of the contents of a previously examined cube face was presented instead of the requested information. Although there were large age differences in the accuracy of the cube comparison decisions, young and old adults were equivalent in the accuracy of recognizing the identity and orientation of the letter in previously examined cube faces.

Several interpretations can be proposed to account for the variations in the pattern of results obtained from the recognition probe procedure when used in different tasks. For instance, the tasks may have varied in the difficulty of the discrimination between same and different information in the recognition test, in the amount of information that had to be remembered, or in the codability of that information. The recognition measures in some of the studies also may have had low reliability because of the small number of probe recognition trials.

Questions also can be raised about the validity of the recognition probe procedure for the assessment of working memory. For example, it is possible that working memory does not contain explicitly presented information, but only information that has been transformed in some manner from the format in which it was originally presented. If this is the case, then the accuracy of recognizing probes of explicitly presented information may be unrelated to the functioning of working memory because the untransformed information might never have been preserved in working memory.

A second complication with the recognition probe procedure is that recognition accuracy can vary for reasons other than the characteristics of one's working memory. As an example, mere intention to use the information in the task could lead to a recognition impairment in older adults. Evidence that something like this may be happening is available in results obtained with a mental synthesis task (Salthouse, Mitchell, & Palmon, 1989). No age differences were found in the accuracy of recognizing relevant information (line patterns) when that information was tested in isolation, but precisely the same information was recognized less accurately by older adults when it was probed in the context of a synthesis task. Little or no difference across the conditions was evident in samples of young adults. This phenomenon, which is apparently reliable because it was observed in two independent experiments, could be interpreted as suggesting that intention or purpose is involved in working memory. Speculations such as this are clearly post hoc, however, and it is not yet clear exactly what information is preserved in working memory during the solution of a cognitive task. Nevertheless, at least some of the results from the recognition probe procedure are consistent with the interpretation that one factor contributing to cognitive difficulties associated with increased age is reduced availability of relevant information while attempting to solve the task.

Several other measures used to investigate age-related differences in working memory also have proved to be ambiguous. An example is the number of redundant or repetitive information requests in successive-presentation versions of the cube comparison and matrix reasoning tasks (Salthouse, under review; Salthouse & Skovronek, in press). A reliable finding, evident in both tasks and across eight independent experiments, is that older adults make more redundant requests than young adults by repeatedly examining the contents of the same cube face or the same matrix cell.

I initially hypothesized that the greater number of redundant information requests reflected a working memory limitation in that there was more loss of early information during subsequent processing among people with ineffective working memory systems, and consequently they had a greater need to reinstate the lost information through repetitive examinations or inspections. However, subsequent research revealed that the number of redundant information requests was not correlated with probe recognition measures of information availability, or with other measures of working memory (i.e., computation span, and a spatial analog termed the *line span*). As a consequence, I now suspect that the number of redundant requests largely reflects a greater desire for confidence before making decisions, and therefore I no longer believe that this measure is very useful as an index of information availability or working memory functioning.

Only a few aspects of working memory have been investigated with experimental analysis techniques. However, the working memory influence could be pervasive, and perhaps manifested as deficits in the creation or maintenance of the internal representations used in many cognitive activities. That is, if a consequence of impaired working memory is that less information can be simultaneously available, then both the quality and the stability of internal representations could be negatively affected. It may even be impossible to solve very complex or abstract problems if the solutions to earlier subparts are not available when they are needed for higher-order processing. I have speculated that something like this may be involved in the age differences found in tasks as diverse as block design (Salthouse, 1987b), series completion (Salthouse & Prill, 1987), geometric analogies (Salthouse, 1987c) and mental synthesis (Salthouse, 1987a; Salthouse & Mitchell, 1989).

CAUSES OF RELATIONS BETWEEN AGE AND WORKING MEMORY

In light of the evidence from both statistical control procedures and experimental analysis procedures that working memory seems to have an important mediating influence on age–cognition relations, it is reasonable to ask what is responsible for the age differences in working memory. Three possibilities have been mentioned in the research literature (see Salthouse, 1990, for a review), and can be represented schematically in terms of the desktop metaphor in which a single surface is temporarily partitioned into regions for storage and processing. These representations are illustrated in Figure 2.16.

The top rectangle portrays the desktop of young adults in which there is a relatively large region that can be allocated to storage or processing. The lower left rectangle, corresponding to a smaller desktop, represents the possibility that people might differ in their storage capacity, such that in some people less space is available for preserving materials, and consequently there is a greater need for frequent exchanges to and from larger and more stable storage systems. The middle rectangle portrays the possibility that individual differences in working memory originate because of variations in processing efficiency, such that in some individuals the processing requires a larger proportion of the available space, thereby leaving a smaller region available for temporary storage. Another possible source of individual differences in working memory relates to the effectiveness with which multiple types of information or processing can be coordinated. One way of representing this interpretation within the desktop metaphor is in terms of the messy or cluttered desk

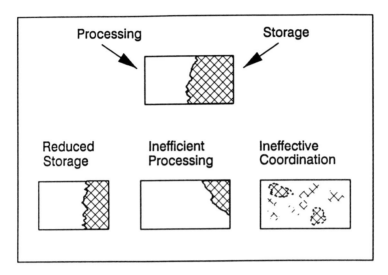

FIGURE 2.16   Schematic representation of three sources of individual differences in working memory according to the desktop metaphor.

represented in the lower right of Figure 2.16. Both processing and
storage could be impaired if there is a blurring of boundaries or
distinctions between the contents of processing and the contents of
storage, leading to confusion between new and old materials.

A project reported by Salthouse and Babcock (1991) was designed
to investigate which of these possibilities was most plausible in
accounting for adult age differences in working memory. The first
study in this project involved 227 adults between 20 and 87 years of
age. The computation span and listening span tasks served as the
criterion working memory tasks in this study, and all research participants also performed a battery of tasks designed to assess each
hypothesized component. Traditional digit and word spans were used
as the measures of storage capacity, and the speed of arithmetic and
the speed of answering sentence comprehension questions when each
was performed alone served as the measures of processing efficiency.
Coordination effectiveness was assessed in terms of the speed of performing arithmetic and the speed of answering sentence comprehension
questions when both tasks were performed simultaneously.

Figure 2.17 reveals that there were significant age-related declines
in the performance measures from each task. The absolute levels of
performance were lower when concurrent processing was required

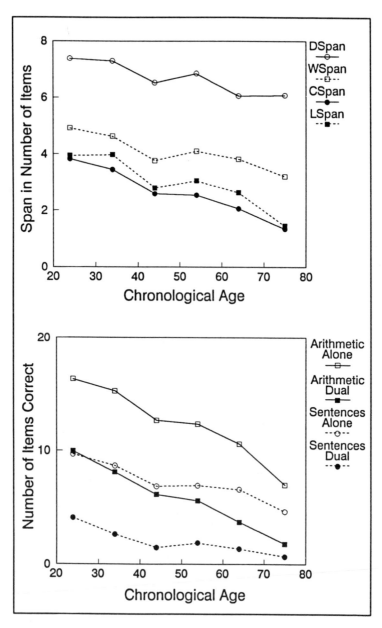

FIGURE 2.17   Mean span performance (top panel), and mean number of items completed in 20 sec (bottom panel) as a function of age decade.

(i.e., the computation span and listening span measures in the top panel, and the dual measures in the bottom panel), but pronounced negative age trends were evident in each measure.

Of greatest interest in this study was the amount of attenuation of the age-related variance in the measures of working memory after controlling measures of different hypothesized components. Results from separate regression analyses conducted with the composite measures derived from the two sets of tasks serving as the potential mediators are summarized in Figure 2.18. Notice that although there was substantial attenuation of the age-related variance after controlling each hypothesized component, the magnitude of the attenuation was greatest (i.e., 93.6%) after controlling the measure of processing efficiency.

In order to pursue this last result, a second study was conducted with even simpler measures of processing efficiency. These measures consisted of the speed of making same/different decisions about pairs

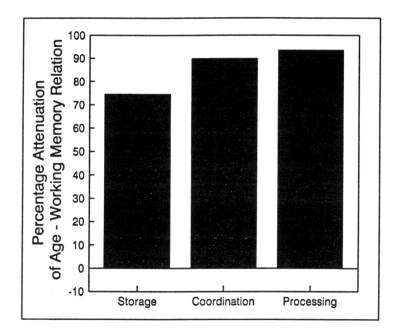

FIGURE 2.18   Percentage attenuation of the relation between age and working memory after statistical control of composite measures of three hypothesized components.

of letters and about pairs of line patterns. A total of 233 adults between 18 and 82 years of age participated in this study. The major results of the second study in the Salthouse and Babcock (1991) project were that the attenuation of the age-related variance in working memory was even greater for the simple perceptual speed measure of processing efficiency (i.e., 96.7%) than for the processing efficiency measures based on the same processing activity required in the working memory tasks (i.e., 91.5%).

Three additional studies, each involving independent samples of 220 or more adults with the same working memory and perceptual speed tasks, were reported in another article published in 1991 (Salthouse, 1991a). The percentages of the attenuation of the age-related variance in working memory in these studies were 82.9%, 94.5%, and 94.2%.

Several other studies with different combinations of working memory measures and processing efficiency or speed measures also have been conducted in my laboratory in the last five years. For example, a study published in 1988 (Salthouse, 1988b) involved 100 young adults and 100 older adults. Backwards Digit Span served as the measure of working memory and the individual's score on the Digit Symbol Substitution Test served as the measure of processing speed. The R^2 associated with age in predicting working memory performance was .123 when it was the only predictor in the regression equation, but this value was reduced to .006, an attenuation of 95.1%, when the speed measure was entered before age in the prediction equation.

In addition, two studies were conducted with the computer-administered versions of the computation span and listening span tasks, and with computer-controlled tasks (computer digit symbol and computer digit digit) used to measure speed (Salthouse, in press-a). The attenuation percentages for the age-related variance in the composite measure of working memory in these studies were 71.3% in a study with 90 young adults and 90 older adults, and 90.4% in a study with 100 adults ranging from 20 to 80 years of age.

Finally, two studies (Salthouse, Babcock, & Shaw, 1991) with small samples of between 30 and 44 adults each in young and old age groups were conducted in which working memory was assessed with a keeping track task similar to that used to introduce the concept of working memory at the beginning of this chapter. Two versions of the keeping track task were presented, one with numbers and addition or subtraction operations, and the other with dot positions and movement or repositioning operations. The percentage attenuation of the age-related variance in these tasks after statistical control of a composite measure of processing speed derived from two computer-administered speed tasks was 88.8% for the numeric version of the task, and 81.7% for the spatial version.

The results of these nine studies, involving a variety of different methods of assessing both working memory and processing speed, are summarized in Figure 2.19. Because statistical control of a measure of processing speed is associated with attenuations of 80% or more of the age-related variance, it can be inferred that some aspect of speed is a major factor in the relations between age and working memory. It is interesting to note that this degree of attenuation corresponds to nearly the same magnitude of shared variance as that evident between two different measures of working memory (i.e., between 66% and 86% overlap of age-related variance with the computation span and listening span measures). The speed at which simple perceptual comparison operations can be performed therefore appears very important as a proximal mediator of age-related influences on working memory, at least when the latter is assessed by tasks requiring simultaneous storage and processing.

How are these results to be interpreted? Why does speed of processing seem to have such an important influence on the age differences in working memory? The interpretation I favor at the current time is as follows. Working memory might be conceptualized as the amount of information that can be kept active at any given time. The effective limit on working memory thus may be dynamic, and related to the rate at which information can be activated, rather than structural, and related to the space available for storage. Instead of considering working memory to be like the surface of a desk, this interpretation suggests that a more appropriate metaphor might be that of a juggler. To be more specific, the functioning of working memory might be analogous to someone trying to juggle items inside a room with a fairly low ceiling. Under conditions such as these, where the presence of a ceiling limits the height of the tosses and gravity serves to ensure that all items drop at the same rate, the primary limit on the number of items that can be kept active is the speed of catching and tossing (i.e., activating) the items.

There are at least two possible sources of individual differences within the dynamic, mental juggling, conceptualization of working

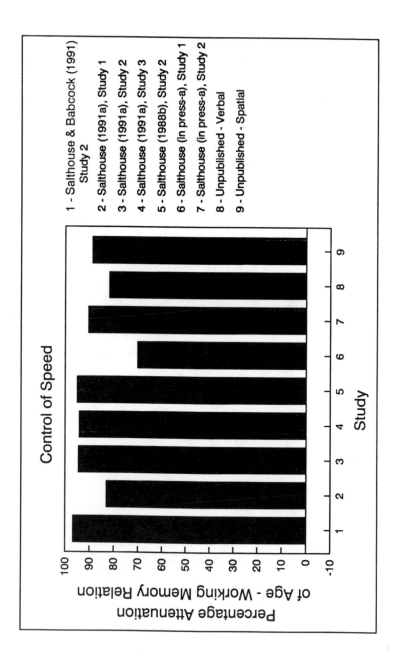

FIGURE 2.19 Percentage attenuation of the relation between age and working memory after statistical control of measures of processing speed.

memory: People might differ in working memory because of differences in the speed at which information is activated, or they might differ because of differences in the rate at which information is lost as a function of time or additional processing. My hypothesis is that the primary age-related differences in working memory are in the speed of activation, and not in the rate at which the information is lost through interference or decay. Evidence from several types of studies indicates that there are little or no age differences in the rate at which information is lost as a function of subsequent processing or additional time. For example, a reliable finding in many continuous recognition memory experiments is that young and old adults have parallel functions relating recognition accuracy to the length of the interval between presentation and test (see Salthouse, in press-a; and Salthouse & Babcock, 1991, for citations). My colleagues and I also have found parallel functions for young and old adults when the number of operations to be performed between presentation and test is manipulated (Salthouse, Babcock, & Shaw, 1991).

There is also considerable evidence that increased age is associated with slower perceptual or encoding processes. Two types of measures that may be particularly relevant to the activation of information in working memory may be described briefly. The first measure is the slope of the function relating subvocal naming time to number of repetitions of the named item. This can be interpreted as providing an estimate of the time required to "activate" or rehearse an internal representation of a single item. Two studies have been conducted with this procedure, one in 1980 (Salthouse, 1980) involving one-syllable words, and the other in 1990 (unpublished) involving digits. The results of both studies were very similar, as the slopes in the 1980 study were .32 sec/item for young adults and .43 sec/item for older adults, while those in the 1990 study were .30 sec/item for young adults and .41 sec/item for older adults. The second measure of activation time was an arithmetic duration threshold obtained by using psychophysical threshold procedures to determine the minimum time needed to perform simple operations of the type involved in the computation span working memory task. In a recent study (Salthouse, in press-a), this measure was found to correlate moderately both with age ($r = .46$) and with a composite measure of perceptual speed ($r = .58$).

There are obviously many ways in which activation time could be assessed, and measures of subvocal naming time or the time required to perform simple arithmetic operations are not necessarily the optimal measures of this construct. It is desirable that other methods of investigating activation time be pursued because a key hypothesis from the present perspective is that working memory differences originate because increased age is associated with slower activation of information for many types of processing.

The proposed interpretation of working memory suggests that working memory tasks may not reflect the operation of a single structure or process, but merely may be tasks in which there are considerable requirements for information processing. Negative relations between age and working memory are hypothesized to occur largely because increased age is associated with a slower rate of activating information. Moreover, because the rate of activation can be assessed with any of a variety of tasks with moderate processing requirements, it is postulated that substantial overlap exists between the age-related variance in tasks presumed to assess working memory and the age-related variance in tasks presumed to assess efficiency or speed of processing. An implication of this view is that processing speed should be considered as a potential mediator of age–cognition relations. That topic is the focus of the next chapter.

Chapter 3
Processing Speed as a Potential Mediator

James Birren (e.g., 1974) was the first theorist to promote the idea that a slower speed of processing might be an important causal factor in the adult age differences in many aspects of cognition. My own interest in speed as a potential mediator of age–cognition relations developed from two different directions. The first impetus for this line of thinking was a review of research on age and speed in which I reached the conclusion that age-related slowing is not due exclusively to sensory and motor processes, but that alterations in the central nervous system also were involved. This led me to suggest that "Since central factors are implicated in the slowing phenomenon, it is reasonable to expect that other cognitive processes will share some of the causes, and perhaps be influenced by the consequences, of age-related slowing (Salthouse, 1985a, p. 421)."

The second influence on my thinking was the intuitive plausibility of influences of speed of processing on cognition. I was, and continue to be, impressed by the idea that a slower speed of processing is likely to mean that the products of earlier processing may not be available by the time later processing is completed. Abstraction, integration, and many other kinds of higher-order processing therefore may be impaired if all the relevant information is not simultaneously available when needed.

These ideas about the influence of processing speed on cognition are related to hypotheses discussed in the field of psychometric intelligence in which speed and intellectual g have been postulated to be related to one another (e.g., Eysenck, 1987; Jensen, 1987; Vernon, 1987). However, speculations of this type can be traced much earlier, as is evident in the following statement by Lemmon in 1927,

> … the most intelligent response is, in general, the one in which the determination of the greatest number of factors have been taken into consideration. In

neural terms this may well mean the response in the determination of which the greatest number of association centers have cooperated, and the number of simultaneously active centers may in turn depend to some extent upon the speed with which nervous impulses are conducted from center to center and through synapses within the centers. (Lemmon, 1927, p. 35)

Although there is controversy about the magnitude of the linkage between processing speed and cognitive functioning in samples of adults with a restricted range of ages, the existence of a substantial correlation between age and measures of processing speed suggests that the consequences of speed variations could be quite large in across-age comparisons. That is, even if there were only small relations between speed and cognition in samples of adults from a narrow range of ages, the relations might be much greater among adults with a broad age variation because of the strong association between age and speed.

AGE–SPEED RELATIONS

I begin the discussion of speed as a potential mediator of age–cognition relations by briefly documenting the relations between age and speed. I reviewed much of the relevant literature in 1985 (Salthouse, 1985a). Two major conclusions from that review were that there were large reliable age effects (i.e., the median age correlation across many different speed variables was .45), and that these effects were not simply attributable to slowed sensory or motor processes. Among the evidence for this latter conclusion was the finding of significant age differences in many derived measures of central processing such as slopes of memory scanning or mental rotation, and assorted difference scores.

I also conducted a few studies of my own to investigate artifactual interpretations of the age-related slowing phenomenon. One study (Salthouse & Somberg, 1982a) was designed to investigate the possibility that the phenomenon might be due to preexperimental differences in the amount of relevant practice. Young and old adults were therefore recruited to perform a choice reaction time task, along with several other tasks, for 50 sessions. The major results of this study, as illustrated in Figure 3.1, were that substantial age differences remained throughout all stages of practice. The apparent implication is that the age-related slowing phenomenon is stable across at least moderate amounts of practice.

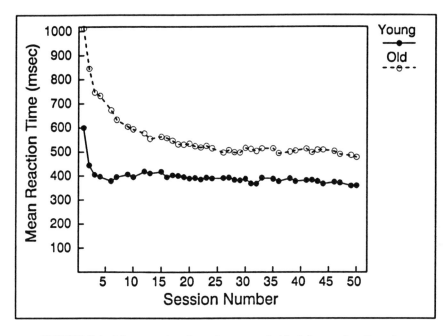

FIGURE 3.1   Mean reaction time of young and old adults as a function of practice. Data omitted from sessions involving transfer conditions.

There was also a suspicion that some of the slowness of the elderly might be a consequence of greater cautiousness as manifested in a bias favoring accuracy over speed. This possibility was investigated by encouraging young and old adults to perform a choice reaction time task at different speeds, and then constructing functions relating speed and accuracy to allow comparisons of speed at the same accuracy (Salthouse & Somberg, 1982b). The results of this study, illustrated in Figure 3.2, indicated pronounced age differences at all levels of accuracy, therefore implying that the slowing phenomenon could not be dismissed as an artifact of a speed–accuracy tradeoff.

Because the administration of cognitive tasks on a computer allows unobtrusive time measurement, young and old adults can be compared in the duration of many hypothesized processing components. In most of these comparisons young adults have been found to have shorter durations, indicating faster speed, than older adults. To illustrate, this was evident in a block design task with measures of the time to evaluate the pattern and the time to select an appropriate manipulation

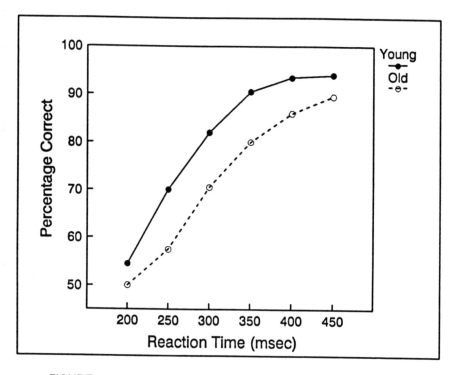

FIGURE 3.2   Mean accuracy at each of six levels of reaction time for young and old adults.

(Salthouse, 1987b), and in a series completion task in the time to encode an element and in the time to identify the relation among elements (Salthouse & Prill, 1987).

Results of the type just described led to the conclusion that the age-related slowing phenomenon is genuine, in that it is not an artifact of low levels of practice or of greater bias toward accuracy, and is pervasive, in that it is evident in a wide range of measures. Whenever a large number of variables exhibit a similar pattern it is tempting to speculate that a common factor might be involved in all of the variables. The primary hypothesis that has guided my research in this area is that there may be one or more relatively general or common speed-of-processing factors that are affected by age-related processes, and that these factors in turn influence the rate of executing many different cognitive operations.

These ideas are represented in Figure 3.3. Four important points should be emphasized in connection with this figure. First, I am not claiming that there is only a single speed factor because I am willing to consider the possibility that there may be multiple speed factors analogous to the existence of multiple cognitive ability factors. However, the number of speed factors clearly must be much smaller than the number of possible measures of speed or else it would not be meaningful to refer to factors or influences common to many variables.

Second, the common or general speed factors are not postulated to be the exclusive cause of age differences in speeded measures. Other factors, such as motivation, relevant experience, and characteristics of the specific task under investigation, are also assumed to contribute to the speed of performance in particular measures, and some of these factors may be related to age independent of the hypothesized general influences.

Third, I am not suggesting that the hypothesized speed factors are universal, because the common influences may not affect all measures. Common or general speed factors must affect a relatively large number of measures or the distinction between general and specific may not

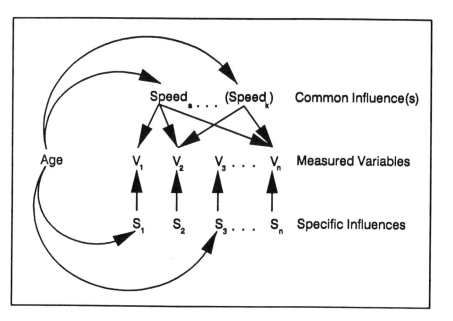

FIGURE 3.3 Hypothesized relations among common and specific age-related influences and measures of speed.

be meaningful, and at some point explanations must be provided for why some measures are affected and others are not. However, I suspect that it is probably too simplistic to expect that all measures assessed in units of time are affected by the factors hypothesized to influence some speed measures.

And fourth, there is no implication that all speed measures will exhibit exactly the same magnitude of age relations. An outcome of this type would only occur if the measures have exactly the same configuration of determinants, and identical weightings of those determinants. Because it is assumed that each measured variable has a somewhat different pattern of common and specific influences, there is no reason to expect that different measures of speed will have similar age trends.

One additional point not represented in the figure but implicit in my perspective is that the hypothesized common speed influences are not stylistic nor reflections of one's personality, but instead are presumed to reflect properties of the central nervous system. I do not have a strong position on the issue of whether the distal causes of the speed differences are endogenous or exogenous, but I do believe that the consequences of those causes are represented biologically, and most likely within the central nervous system.

This perspective implies that all speed measures can be assumed to reflect a constellation of influences because they are a product both of determinants common to other measures, and of determinants specific to that measure. The strategy that I have pursued has been to examine the influence of this constellation on age–cognition relations by means of statistical control procedures, and after discovering that some speed measures do appear to function as an important mediator of these relations, then to try to disentangle the contributions of each aspect of speed.

SELECTION OF BEST MEASURE OF SPEED

In order to use statistical control procedures to investigate the mediational role of speed in age–cognition relations, it is necessary to identify an appropriate measure of speed. As discussed above, all speed measures can be assumed to have multiple determinants including error, specific influences, and possibly one or more common influences related to the speed of performing many mental operations. The important question in this context is: What are the best measures to emphasize the hypothesized common influences?

The optimum measure of processing speed should neither be too simple nor too complex. It should not be too simple because this may overemphasize the sensory and motor aspects relative to the aspects hypothesized to reflect the rate of executing mental operations. Simple reaction time, and tasks requiring fine sensory discriminations or precise motor responses, therefore are probably not the most appropriate measures to assess the hypothesized common speed influences.

The optimum speed measure also should not be too complex because then the measures may be influenced substantially by the type of processing being performed or the content of what is being processed, in which case the measures may represent cognitive ability or knowledge factors more than the speed at which many operations can be performed. Solution times in cognitive tasks therefore seem unsuitable as measures of the hypothesized processing speed factor (or factors).

The most desirable measure is probably that from the simplest task in which the performance measure has plausibility as an index of the speed of mental operations. This most likely will come from tasks that would be performed perfectly if there were no time constraints, but which involve a number of elementary mental operations such as comparison or substitution. Promising candidates that appear to satisfy these criteria are measures of what are referred to as perceptual speed.

Several perceptual speed tasks used in my projects are illustrated in Figure 3.4. The pattern comparison task involves same/different judgments about pairs of patterns, each containing either three, six, or nine line segments. Responses are communicated by writing an S (for Same) or a D (for Different) on the line between the pair of patterns. The letter comparison task involves same/different judgments about pairs of letter strings, each containing either three, six, or nine letters. As in the pattern comparison task, responses are communicated by writing an S (for Same) or a D (for Different) on the line between the pair of letters.

Although not represented in Figure 3.4, I have also used the Digit Symbol Substitution Test from the Wechsler Adult Intelligence Scale–Revised (Wechsler, 1981) to measure perceptual speed. This test

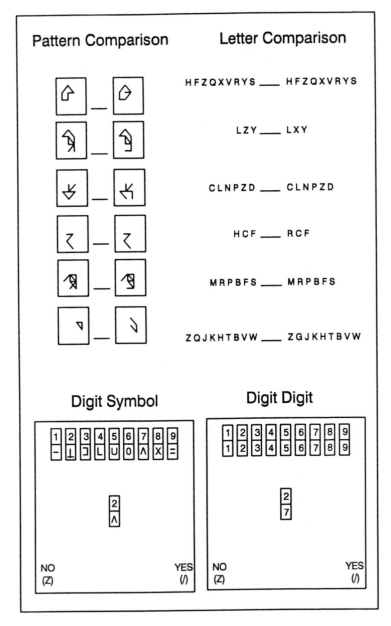

FIGURE 3.4 Illustration of perceptual speed tasks used in several projects. The top two tasks were administered with paper-and-pencil procedures, and the bottom two tasks were administered on a computer.

consists of a code table relating digits to symbols, and rows of double boxes with a digit in the top box and nothing in the bottom box. The task is to write the symbols that are associated with the digits in the code table in the empty box below each digit. The score is the number of symbols written correctly in 90 sec.

Two computer-administered tests have been developed based on the Digit Symbol Substitution Test (Salthouse, in press-b) and are illustrated in the bottom of Figure 3.4. Each test requires a series of binary decisions and key press responses. One key is to be pressed if the members of the pair match according to the code table (digit symbol test), or according to physical identity (digit digit test), and another key is to be pressed if the members of the pair do not match.

Figure 3.5 illustrates the relations between age and performance on these measures with each decade represented by about 150 adults with the paper-and-pencil measures and by about 40 adults with the com-

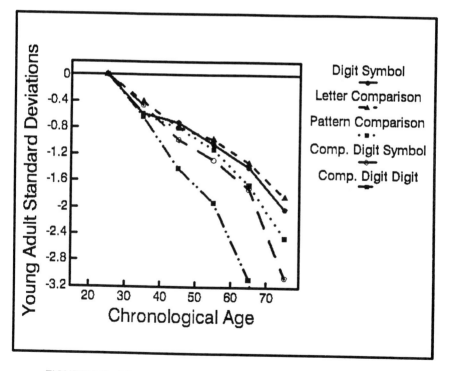

FIGURE 3.5   Mean performance, in young adult standard deviation units, across age decades for five measures of perceptual speed.

puter-administered measures. Correlations with age in several samples (Salthouse, in press-a, in press-b, in preparation) with wide age ranges were –.51, –.54, and –.61 for the Digit Symbol measure, –.59 and –.65 for the pattern comparison measure, –.51 and –.56 for the letter comparison measure, .61 for the computer digit symbol measure, and .54 for the computer digit digit measure. (Correlations for the latter two measures are positive rather than negative because they are assessed in units of time per response rather than in number of items answered correctly in the allotted time.)

These measures also are correlated highly with each other, and with other measures of perceptual speed. As an example, the correlations between the pattern comparison and letter comparison measures were .74 and .78 in two studies with sample sizes of 305 (Salthouse, in preparation) and 913 (Salthouse, in press-b), respectively. Other correlations were .63 and .70 between the Digit Symbol and pattern comparison measures, .64 and .69 between the Digit Symbol and letter comparison measures, and .73 between the paper-and-pencil Digit Symbol measure and the computer-administered digit symbol measure.

Correlations of this magnitude indicate that about 40% to 50% of the total variance in one of the measures is shared with the other measure. Of greater importance for the present purposes, however, is the percentage of common age-related variance across the measures. Estimates of the percentages of shared age-related variance derived from statistical control procedures (see Figure 2.3 for the reasoning involved in these procedures) range from 72% to 99%. To illustrate, in two studies with 910 and 305 research participants, the age-related variance in the Digit Symbol measure was reduced by 98.7% and 92.7% when a composite of pattern comparison and letter comparison performance was statistically controlled (Salthouse, in press-b, in preparation).

To summarize, perceptual speed measures seem to possess many desirable characteristics as an index of at least one of the hypothesized speed-of-processing factors. The tasks are quite simple, and yet operations such as comparison and substitution have at least some cognitive aspects. These measures have large correlations with one another, implying that they are assessing a common construct, and have a very large proportion of shared age-related variance, indicating that they also are highly similar with respect to age-related influences.

Measures of perceptual speed therefore appear to be reasonable choices to serve as potential mediators of age–cognition relations in statistical control analyses.

STATISTICAL CONTROL OF SPEED

Some early results of using statistical control procedures with perceptual speed measures as the controlled variable in the examination of relations between age and various measures of cognitive functioning were summarized in a book published in 1985 (Salthouse, 1985b). The methods used in those initial analyses were weak because the samples were generally small, and almost always involved two extreme groups rather than a continuous range of ages. Furthermore, only single variables were used in the assessment of both cognition and speed. The results of those analyses were far from convincing, but they nevertheless were encouraging to someone who already had strong interest in the hypothesis that speed factors might be important in mediating the relations between age and cognition.

Much stronger evidence for the speed-mediation hypothesis was reported in two studies by Hertzog (1989) and Schaie (1989). These researchers found that the attenuation of the relations between age and relatively simple measures of cognition after statistical control of composite measures of perceptual speed ranged from 77% to 91%.

In the last several years I have been involved in a total of 10 studies in which relatively large numbers of adults of different ages have been administered various cognitive tests and tests of perceptual speed. Many of these studies have not previously been analyzed using statistical control procedures based on composite measures of speed and cognition, and thus appropriate reanalyses have been conducted so that all of the results could be expressed in the same format.

Two studies were reported in 1988 (Salthouse, 1988b) in which the primary measure of speed was the score from the Digit Symbol Substitution Test. One study involved 100 young adults and 100 older adults who each performed four cognitive tasks: mental synthesis, paper folding, and two versions of a geometric analogies task. Because both time and accuracy were emphasized, an integrated performance index was created by averaging the z-scores for the accuracy and time (reflected) values in each task. These indexes then were averaged across the four cognitive tasks to form a single composite measure of cognitive functioning. Age was associated with an R^2 of .428 in the regression equation predicting the composite cognition measure, but this value was reduced to .116 after statistically controlling the variance associated with the Digit Symbol speed measure. This is equivalent to an attenuation of the age-related variance of 72.9%.

The second study in the 1988 project was very similar except that there were only 40 older adults and 100 young adults, and only two cognitive tasks were performed, mental synthesis and geometric analogies. Results of this study were nearly identical to those of the first study because the R^2 associated with age in the prediction of composite cognition was .437, and this was reduced to .027, an attenuation of 93.8%, after statistical control of the Digit Symbol measure.

A study conducted in collaboration with Donald Kausler and Scott Saults (Salthouse, Kausler, & Saults, 1988) was administered completely on computers. A total of 233 adults between 20 and 79 years of age performed two reasoning tasks, geometric analogies and number series completion, and two modified versions of common perceptual speed tasks, digit symbol substitution and number comparison. When considered alone, age was associated with an R^2 of .305 in the prediction of a composite measure of time and accuracy in the two reasoning tasks, but the age-related variance was reduced by 64.9%, to .107, after controlling the variance associated with the composite measure of speed.

Standard paper-and-pencil tests of cognition were used in a study reported by Salthouse and Mitchell (1990). The 383 adults in this study performed the Shipley Abstraction Test, and five tests from the ETS Kit of Cognitive Tests—Letter Sets, Paper Folding, and Surface Development to measure cognition, and Finding As and Number Comparison to measure perceptual speed. This sample may have been somewhat unusual because the relations between age and speed, and between age and specific measures of cognition, were smaller than those found in other studies. To illustrate, the proportion of age-related variance in the speed measure in this study was only .078 compared to values of .261 to .577 in other studies, and the proportion of age-related variance in the Shipley Abstraction measure was only .063 compared to .221 in another recent study (Salthouse, 1991a, Study 1). Despite what may be an atypical sample, statistical control of the perceptual speed measure reduced the proportion of age-associated variance in the composite cognition measure from .124 to .055, corresponding to an attenuation of 55.6%.

Three relevant studies were reported in an article published in 1991 (Salthouse, 1991a). Over 220 adults between 20 and 84 years of age participated in each study, and the pattern comparison and letter comparison perceptual speed tasks were performed by all participants. The cognitive tests in one study were the Raven's Advanced Progressive Matrices and the Shipley Abstraction Test, and the same four tasks—integrative reasoning, geometric analogies, paper folding, and cube assembly—were used in the other two studies. Composite measures of cognition and speed were derived in each study and analyzed with multiple regression procedures. The proportions of age-related variance in the cognitive measure before control of the speed measure were .305, .169, and .255, respectively, in Studies 1, 2, and 3, and the corresponding proportions after control of speed were .044, .011, and .037. The attenuation percentages in the three studies were therefore 85.6%, 93.5%, and 85.5%.

Another study published in 1991 (Salthouse, 1991c) involved the administration of four computer-controlled tests of spatial visualization to 132 adults between 21 and 80 years of age. Age was associated with an R^2 of .119 in the prediction of a composite measure of performance across the four cognitive tests, but the proportion of age-related variance after statistical control of a composite of the computer digit symbol and computer digit digit speed measures was only .023. This is equivalent to an attenuation of 80.7%.

A total of 305 adults from a wide range of ages performed four cognitive tests and seven perceptual speed tests in a recently completed study (Salthouse, in preparation). The cognitive tests were the Space and Reasoning tests from the Schaie–Thurstone Adult Mental Abilities Test (Schaie, 1985), and the integrative reasoning and geometric analogies tests used in Studies 2 and 3 of the Salthouse (1991a) project. The perceptual speed tests involved a range of operations such as comparison, substitution, and transformation, and included the Digit Symbol Substitution Test and both the pattern comparison and letter comparison tests. When age was the only variable in the equation predicting composite cognition, it was associated with an R^2 of .202, but the increment in R^2 associated with age after the composite index of speed had been entered into the equation was only .003. The attenuation of the age–cognition relations in this study was therefore 98.5%.

A final relevant study is a doctoral dissertation conducted by Renee Babcock under my supervision. She tested 183 adults between 21 and 83 years of age, each of whom performed five cognitive tests and three perceptual speed tests. The cognitive tests were the Raven's Advanced Progressive Matrices Test, and four cognitive tests from the ETS Kit of Cognitive Tests—Letter Sets, Figure Classification, Calendar, and Following Directions. Two of the perceptual speed tests were also from the ETS Kit—Identical Pictures and Number Comparison; the third perceptual speed test was the Digit Symbol Substitution Test. The attenuation of the age–cognition relations after statistical control of the composite speed measure was 96.6%, corresponding to a reduction in age-associated variance from .178 to .006.

The results of the ten studies just described are summarized in Figure 3.6. The striking feature of these data is that similar results are apparent across the ten independent studies despite quite different measures of speed and cognition. There is some variation in the magnitude of the attenuation, which may be related to sample characteristics or to the particular combination of speed and cognitive measures employed in a given study. However, the attenuation was always 50% or more, and therefore these results indicate that speed is definitely in the important to major range in terms of the magnitude of its influence as a potential mediator of the relations between age and cognition.

It is perhaps not surprising that the speed-related influences are large with easy cognitive tests in which the difficulty level of the items is low, but the influences are also moderately large with measures that can be considered to assess cognitive power, such as the Raven's Advanced Progressive Matrices Test. Moreover, the speed influence is not simply an artifact of the use of timed cognitive tests because similar patterns are evident when performance is assessed in terms of the percentage of attempted items answered correctly. For example, control of speed was associated with attenuations of the age-related variance in composite percentage-correct measures of 70.7% to 91.3% in the three studies reported by Salthouse (1991a), compared to attenuations with a composite measure of number of correctly answered items of between 85.5% and 93.5%.

Evidence of speed mediation of age–cognition relations also is

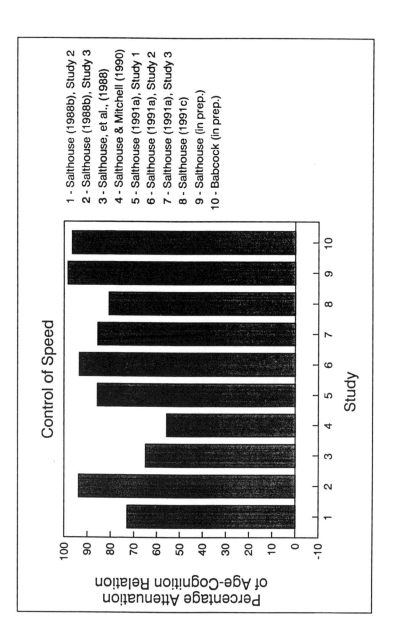

FIGURE 3.6 Percentage attenuation of the relation between age and cognition after statistical control of measures of perceptual speed.

apparent in measures of accuracy obtained from self-paced tasks. For example, three studies were conducted in which matrix reasoning tasks were presented on a computer in a manner that allowed the research participants to take as long as they wanted to inspect the stimuli and make their decisions. In addition, computer speed measures (digit symbol and digit digit) were obtained from each individual (Salthouse, under review). Results from these studies are not represented in Figure 3.6 because there was only a single measure of cognitive functioning (accuracy in the matrix reasoning decisions) and the samples were relatively small (i.e., only 30 young adults and 30 older adults in each study). However, the results appear to be reliable because the same basic pattern was evident in three independent studies employing slightly different procedures. Estimates of the speed-mediated attenuations of the age-related variance in matrix decision accuracy derived from statistical control procedures in these three studies were 82.1%, 70.4%, and 85.1%.

Additional results in the Salthouse, et al. (1988) study suggested that the attenuation of the age-related influences might be considerably smaller with memory measures, such as those based on paired associates and span tasks, than with cognitive measures such as those assessing inductive reasoning. That is, the attenuation of the age-associated variance was only 28.2% for a composite memory measure compared to 64.9% for a composite cognitive measure. This apparent discrepancy in the magnitude of attenuation of age relations led to further investigation of the role of speed in mediating relations between age and memory. Two recent studies therefore involved the administration of paired associate and free recall memory tests in addition to paper-and-pencil tests of perceptual speed.

In one of the studies (Salthouse, in preparation), involving 305 adults from a wide range of ages, the R^2 for age in prediction of composite memory performance was .184, and the age-associated variance was reduced to .032 after statistical control of the speed composite. This attenuation of 82.6% is somewhat less than that found for the cognitive measures in this same study (i.e., 98.5%), but it is still quite substantial. The second study (unpublished) involved 77 young adults and 69 older adults. The age-associated variance in the composite memory measure in this study was reduced from .616 to .060, corresponding to an attenuation of 90.3%. At least based on the evidence from these two studies, therefore, it appears that the attenuation of age-related influences on memory is quite large, although possibly slightly smaller than that evident in other measures of cognitive functioning. However, definitive conclusions regarding the relative magnitude of speed mediation across different types of cognition such as memory abilities versus reasoning or spatial abilities are premature because the amount of relevant data is still very limited.

HOW DOES SLOWER SPEED OF PROCESSING AFFECT QUALITY OF COGNITIVE PERFORMANCE?

In light of the impressive results from the statistical control procedures it appears appropriate to pursue the next step in the proposed investigative strategy—relying on experimental analytical procedures to determine the mechanisms by which age is related to speed, and by which speed is related to cognition. Unfortunately, no direct evidence is available from experimental manipulations because it is not yet obvious how the internal rate of processing can be altered. Stimulus presentation time and the time allowed for a response can be varied, but it is unlikely that these manipulations affect the rate at which internal processing operations are executed. There have been some attempts to simulate the effects of slower processing by variations of the stimulus material (e.g., number of syllables in the to-be-remembered words in Salthouse, 1980), but this manipulation probably has limited applicability because it is likely to affect only a few aspects of processing (e.g., processes concerned with subvocal rehearsal). Although physiological state might be altered with certain drugs, inducement of fatigue, and so forth, it is not clear that processing speed, and only processing speed, would be affected by these manipulations. The lack of evidence from experimental studies is disappointing, but analytical experimental procedures are simply not very useful when the critical variables cannot be directly manipulated.

Although the absence of convincing experimental evidence precludes strong conclusions, it is nonetheless possible to offer some speculations about how slower processing speed might lead to lower levels of cognitive functioning. First, with simple tests of cognition, of the type referred to as speed tests, it seems reasonable to conjecture that performance is primarily determined by the number of items that can be completed in the available time because of the low difficulty level of the items. Speed thus can be postulated to exert a direct influence on performance in simple cognitive tests. In more complex or difficult cognitive tests, of the power variety, much of the speed influence may be indirect, and possibly mediated through decreased efficiency of working memory and reductions in the amount of information that can be kept simultaneously active. The highest levels of abstraction or integration therefore may not be attainable because the products of early processing are lost before later processing is completed. A slower rate of processing also may lead to ineffectiveness of some strategies, and consequently to adjustments and accommodations in the nature of the processing carried out. The speed influence on memory might be similar to that hypothesized with respect to complex cognition, although it is possible that nonspeed factors exert a greater influence on memory measures than on other types of cognitive measures.

REFINING THE NATURE OF THE SPEED MEDIATOR

It seems likely that knowledge of the relations between speed and cognition will accumulate more rapidly when there is a better understanding of the types of speed that are affected by increased age, and how each type contributes to the relation between age and cognition. Two issues are especially important in this connection. One is whether the speed involved in mediating age–cognition relations is relatively general, and common to many speed variables, or is highly specific, and limited to a few critical variables. The second issue is whether distinct speed factors can be identified, and if so, whether they differ in terms of their mediational influence on age–cognition relations.

As noted earlier, a key assumption of my perspective is that age-related effects on most measures of speed reflect a combination of both general and specific influences. In this context, general means that the influences are common to many measures, and specific means that they are restricted to a few highly similar measures. Because the use of composite speed measures is presumed to emphasize the general aspects, I have hypothesized that general or common speed factors play a major role in mediating age–cognition relations. It is

nevertheless desirable to explore other means of distinguishing between general and specific age-related speed influences.

One possible method relies on the existence of systematic relations
among the age differences across a variety of speed variables. The
rationale underlying this method is as follows. If only unique or
specific determinants are responsible for the effects of age on each
variable, and there are no shared or common age-related influences,
then there is no reason to expect a correlation between the magnitude
of the age differences across a range of variables. In other words, if
the age difference in variable V_1 is determined by different factors than
the age difference in variable V_2, then no relation would be expected
between the age differences in the two variables. However, if many
variables are affected by the same age-related influence, then a
moderate to high correlation would be expected between the magnitude of the age differences across a set of variables because the age
differences are at least partially determined by a shared factor. That is,
if the age differences in V_1 and V_2 are both influenced by a general
factor in addition to miscellaneous specific factors, then the age
differences in the two variables should be related because of the
influence they have in common.

This reasoning can be elaborated by reference to Figure 3.7. (Also
see Salthouse, in press-e, for further discussion of this argument.) The
graphs in this figure consist of plots of the average time of older adults
on a given variable against the average time of young adults on that
same variable. Both axes are on the same scale and hence the positive
diagonal, represented by the dotted line, corresponds to equivalent
levels of performance in the two groups. When age differences are
present they can be characterized in terms of the deviation of the
observed data point from the positive diagonal. Deviations can be
expressed relative to either axis, but because it is more common to
represent the dependent or measured variable along the vertical axis,
the performance of older adults is linked to that of young adults by
differences portrayed in the vertical axis.

If the age differences in each variable are determined by specific or
unique influences, then the age differences in one variable should be
independent of those in other variables. This situation is represented
in panel (A), where there is no systematic relation between the
magnitude of the age difference (vertical deviation) in one variable
and those in other variables. Independence of the size of the age

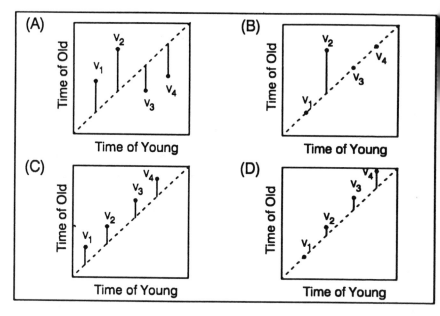

FIGURE 3.7   Illustration of four possible patterns of the times of older adults as a function of the times of young adults.

differences across different variables implies an absence of a correlation between the average times in the two groups.

However, the situation portrayed in panel (A) is probably too extreme because the differences in some variables (i.e., V_3 and V_4) are below the positive diagonal, and thus imply that older adults were faster than young adults on these measures. A more realistic situation may be that portrayed in panel (B), in which the specific age-related influence corresponds to age differences favoring young adults in a small number of variables, with no differences between young and old adults in the remaining variables. This type of pattern likely would lead to a positive correlation between the average times in the two groups, with the magnitude of the correlation dependent on the size of the specific influence, on the relative time of the critical variable, and on the number of variables in the data set with each type of influence.

There are at least two other ways in which the correlation between the average times of young and old adults could be high when there are differences between the two groups. Both of these possibilities, which are represented in panels (C) and (D), are consistent with the existence of a common factor influencing the age differences in many measures. In panel (C) the correlation would be high because the magnitude of the age difference is constant across all variables. A pattern of this type might be produced by a common influence that was present to the same degree in all tasks. The correlation also would be high in panel (D), in this case because the magnitude of the age differences increases in approximate proportion to the average value of the measure in the group of young adults. A pattern of this type might be produced by a factor whose influence was roughly proportional to the total duration of the task.

An advantage of analyzing data in this fashion is that the parameters of the regression equation relating the average times of older adults to the average times of young adults can be examined to determine the manner in which the hypothesized common factor exerts its influence. (Linear relations between the two sets of times are assumed for simplicity, and because this appears to provide a good approximation to the empirical patterns.) For example, if there are no age differences in any of the variables, then all of the deviations will be zero, and because this is equivalent to the positive diagonal in the graphs, the intercept will be zero and the slope will be one. However, if differences do occur, then they might be manifested in the intercept parameter, in the slope parameter, or in both parameters. The simplest cases of effects on a single parameter are illustrated in Figure 3.7. Panel (A) represents the absence of a systematic relation, and is distinguished by a low correlation. Data of the type portrayed in panel (C) would be characterized by an intercept greater than zero and a slope of approximately one, whereas the pattern in panel (D) implies an intercept close to zero and a slope greater than one. The outcome represented in panel (B) is ambiguous because, as noted above, the particular regression parameters affected depends on the magnitude of the specific influence, the range of times for the variables within each category, and the number of variables of each type. For example, if the times of the critical variables are long, then the slope is likely to be greater than one, but if the critical times are short, then the effect may be manifested as an intercept greater than zero.

Even without the ambiguity inherent in alternative (B), one should expect it to be difficult to distinguish among these alternatives because of the large number of determinants of performance speed, and because of the possibility (likelihood?) that the combination of determinants varies across sets of measures. It is also well known that regression analyses are sensitive to the range of observations in both sets of variables, and hence the estimates may be misleading if the measurement range is restricted in one or both groups. Finally, the confidence intervals around each observation are likely to be large when there are either a small number of observations per individual, a small number of individuals per group, or both small numbers of observations and of research participants. It is obviously difficult to discriminate among possible alternatives if the region encompassing the 95% confidence interval around each data point allows many possible fits to the data.

Despite these potential problems, many analyses have revealed that there are often systematic relations between the speeds of young and old adults, and that the regression functions tend to have high correlations, small intercepts, and slopes greater than one (Salthouse, 1985a, 1985b). It is important to emphasize that this characterization is a descriptive generalization (Salthouse, 1991b), or an abstract description of the results of several analyses. Exceptions to this pattern can and do exist (Salthouse, 1988c), and the pattern by itself does not in any way constitute an explanation of age-related slowing phenomena.

These systematic relations can be illustrated with results from a recently completed project (Salthouse, in preparation). Eleven paper-and-pencil speeded tasks were performed by 100 college students (ages 19 to 27), who served as a reference group, and by 305 adults between 19 and 84 years of age. The tasks were intended to represent a wide range of processing demands, and included making horizontal or vertical marks on lines, copying digits or letters, comparing letters, digits, or line patterns, transforming letters or digits, and substituting symbols for digits. Scores in each task were converted into units of seconds per item, and then regression functions relating times of an individual (or of a group) to the mean times in the reference group were computed.

Figure 3.8 illustrates the type of results obtained from these analyses. This figure represents the mean times of adults in their 60s plotted against the mean times of the reference group of college students. Notice that the correlation between the two sets of times is high, the intercept is close to zero, and the slope is greater than one. These are the characteristics associated with the pattern represented in panel (D) of Figure 3.7.

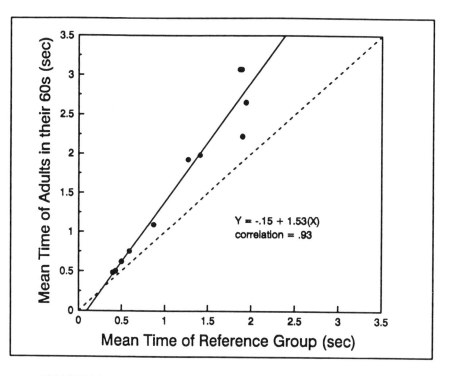

FIGURE 3.8   Plot of mean times of adults in their 60s against the mean times of a reference group of college students.

The regression functions also can be examined as a function of the age of the individual. Figure 3.9 illustrates the regression functions for the mean times at each decade from the 20s through the 70s. There are two prominent features of the data portrayed in Figure 3.9—the slopes increase with age, and the intercepts decrease with age. Both of these patterns are evident as well in the results based on the functions computed separately for each individual research participant, as the correlations with age were .30 for the slope parameter and −.19 for the intercept parameter.

The increase in the slope and decrease in the intercept occur because there is relatively little age-related difference in the measures with the shortest times (e.g., line marking and copying), but large age-related influences on the measures with the longest times (e.g., substitution and comparison). The lengthier times primarily tend to affect the slope of the regression function, whereas the shorter times have more of an

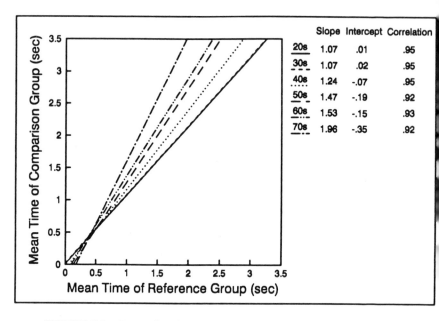

FIGURE 3.9 Regression lines, and parameters, for the mean performance of each age decade as a function of the mean performance of a reference group of college students.

effect on the intercept. The trend for the intercept to become progressively more negative with increased age therefore may be a consequence of an effective axis of rotation above the zero point because the age-related influences are smaller on the fast times than on the slow times. These results are consistent with a proposal by Cerella (1985) that negative intercepts in these types of functions originate because of greater age-related slowing for (relatively slow) cognitive processes than for (relatively fast) sensory and motor processes.

Systematic patterns such as those illustrated in Figures 3.8 and 3.9 can be interpreted as evidence for the existence of a relatively general age-related influence common to many speed variables. That is, high correlations indicate that knowledge of the age difference in one variable is informative about the magnitude of the age difference in other variables, thereby suggesting that the age-related influences in those variables are not independent of one another. Moreover, because the empirical patterns generally reveal that the slope of these functions tends to increase with age, it is frequently considered the most interesting parameter available from these kinds of analyses.

What is not yet clear, however, is what the slope parameter actually represents. Two possible interpretations are portrayed schematically in Figure 3.10. The possibility illustrated in panel (A) is that the slope may be a direct index of one of the hypothesized general speed factors. According to this perspective, the age differences are more pronounced in variables with longer times because more processing operations are involved in variables with longer times, and each operation can be assumed to be slowed by the same relative amount. The slope therefore might be interpreted as corresponding to the (relative) rate of a central timing mechanism, and hence could be viewed as a comparatively pure indicator of (one of) the hypothesized general slowing factor(s).

An alternative interpretation is represented in panel (B). In this case the slope is postulated to be only an indirect index of the general factor, or of multiple specific factors. That is, the slope could be interpreted as simply reflecting the relation among variables that are each affected by a mixture of various types of influences. Age differences might be largest on the slowest measures either because those measures have the greatest susceptibility to a large number of distinct influences, or because they are affected by the most powerful specific influences. Regardless why the absolute magnitude of the age differences varies across variables, however, a key implication of this perspective is that the slope is a less direct indicator of (one of) the hypothesized general speed-of-processing factor(s) than many of the observed variables used in the computation of the slope.

One means by which these two interpretations might be distinguished involves comparing the degree of attenuation of the age–cognition relations across different measures of speed. The primary prediction is that the attenuation associated with the slope parameter should be larger than that associated with the observed measures if it is a direct index of a common speed factor presumed to be involved in the age–cognition relation. However, the slope parameter might be expected to be associated with a relatively small attenuation of the age–cognition relation if the slope merely reflects the relation among variables that are each influenced by an unknown mixture of both general and specific age-dependent and age-independent factors.

Values of the percentage attenuation of the age–cognition relations with the speed measures in the Salthouse (in preparation) study are summarized in Figure 3.11. The most important aspect of these data

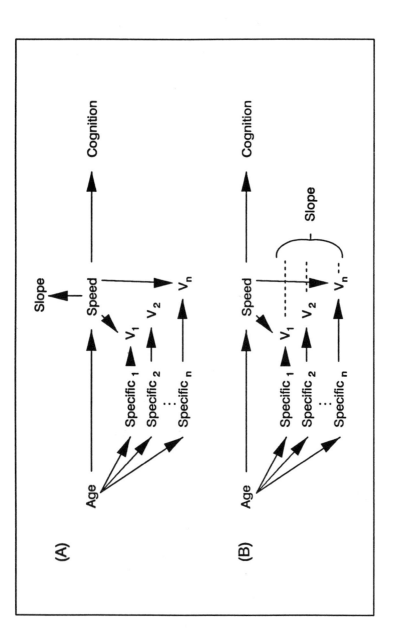

FIGURE 3.10 Schematic representations of alternative interpretations of the slope parameter from regression analyses of the times in two groups.

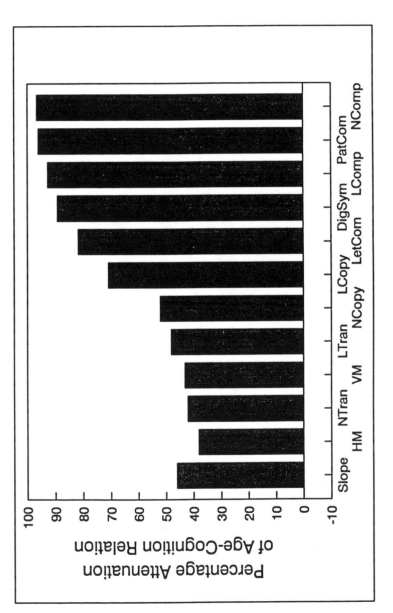

FIGURE 3.11 Percentage attenuation of the relation between age and cognition for different speed measures in the Salthouse (in preparation) study.

with respect to distinguishing between the two interpretations of the slope parameter is the finding that the attenuation of the age–cognition relations associated with statistical control of the slope parameter is smaller than that associated with many of the observed variables. On the basis of the argument outlined earlier, this suggests that the slope parameter is, at best, an indirect indicator of the hypothesized general speed factor. The slope therefore might be most appropriately conceptualized as a byproduct of a constellation of many kinds of determinants across a variety of speed variables, and not as a direct or pure measure of a general speed factor.

Although it initially appeared promising, I now have some reservations about the usefulness of the method of examining relations among variables for distinguishing between general and specific age-related influences on speed. There are two major reasons for the moderation of my enthusiasm. The first is that the method may not be very sensitive to specific effects if the specific age-related influences are small either in absolute terms, or relative to any general age-related influences that might exist. For example, the method is clearly not ideal if the alternative illustrated in panel (B) of Figure 3.7 can't be reliably distinguished from the alternatives illustrated in panels (C) and (D). The second reason for my ambivalence toward the method of systematic relations as a means of distinguishing between general and specific age-related influences is that contrary to speculation, the slope does not seem to have special status as a direct indicator of the hypothesized general speed factor. That is, because the attenuation of the relations between age and cognition was greater after statistical control of many of the observed variables than after control of the slope variable, there is little evidence that the slope is a better, or purer, measure of the hypothesized general factor than are the actual measures from many speeded tasks.

The issue of whether the speed involved in mediating age–cognition relations is general or specific therefore remains undecided. Because of the great variety of speed measures used across the studies summarized in Figure 3.6 and those reported by Hertzog (1989) and Schaie (1989), it appears unlikely that the relevant speed is specific to a few particular measures. Moreover, the use of composite speed measures based on the aggregation of two or more measures also suggests that the speed influences involved in the age–cognition relations are not highly specific. Nevertheless, convincing evidence for an influence of general factors, independent of specific factors, is not yet available.

PERCEPTUAL OR MOTOR SPEED

The results illustrated in Figure 3.11 suggest that the degree of attenuation of the age–cognition relations varies considerably across different speed measures. This raises the question of what kind of speed is involved in the mediation of the relations between age and cognition. One basis for distinguishing among measures of speed is according to whether the measures primarily reflect perceptual or motor processes. That is, all measures require a motor response, but they can be postulated to vary in the relative importance of motor factors because some measures have very minimal cognitive demands (e.g., crossing lines, or copying letters or digits), and others have more appreciable cognitive demands (e.g., substitution or transformation). Performance on perceptual speed tasks therefore might be hypothesized to be influenced by sensory and motor processes and also by factors associated with the execution of simple cognitive operations.

Three studies have been conducted in which measures of both motor speed and perceptual speed, in addition to measures of cognition, were obtained from each research participant. One study involved a composite of time and accuracy in geometric analogies and mental synthesis tasks as the measure of cognition, score on the Digit Symbol Substitution Test as the measure of perceptual speed, and score on a Symbol Copying Test as the measure of motor speed (Salthouse, 1988b, Study 3). Participants in this study consisted of 100 young adults and 40 older adults. The R^2 associated with age in the prediction of the cognition measure was .437, and this was reduced to .071 after control of the motor speed measure, to .027 after control of the perceptual speed measure, and to .017 after control of both measures. Commonality analyses based on the reasoning illustrated in Figure 2.10 were conducted to partition the speed variance into unique and common components. Estimates of the common and unique contributions to the variance shared between age and cognition from the values just reported are .356 for the common influence, .054 unique to perceptual speed, and .010 unique to motor speed.

The study described earlier (Salthouse, in preparation) in which 305 adults performed eleven speed tests in addition to four cognitive tests also provides relevant data because the speed measures can be classified as primarily motoric (i.e., marking lines, and copying letters or digits), or as also involving perceptual or cognitive operations (i.e., comparison, substitution, and transformation). The proportion of the cognition variance associated with age was .202 when age was the only variable in the equation, .080 when motor speed was controlled, .003 when perceptual speed was controlled, and .005 when both motor speed and perceptual speed were controlled. The corresponding variance estimates are .124 for the common influence, .075 unique to perceptual speed, and essentially zero (–.002) unique to motor speed.

A third relevant study is Babcock's (in preparation) doctoral dissertation because in addition to the five cognitive measures and the three perceptual speed measures, all of the participants in this study also performed two line marking tests that can be interpreted as assessing motor speed. The age-associated variance in cognition was .178 when age was considered by itself, .105 after control of motor speed, .006 after control of perceptual speed, and .008 after control of both motor speed and perceptual speed. The estimated contributions were therefore .075 for the common influence, .097 unique to perceptual speed, and essentially zero (–.002) for motor speed.

Figure 3.12 illustrates the results of these three studies in a pie chart format. The total pie represents the overlap of all speed measures with age and cognition (corresponding to the combined area of regions b, c, and d in Figure 2.10). Notice that the common variance is always relatively large, and that perceptual speed is associated with much more unique variance than motor speed. An implication of these results is that motor speed and perceptual speed have a great deal of variance in common, but that perceptual speed appears to be more important than motor speed with respect to mediating the relations between age and cognition.

Another way to represent the simultaneous influence of several variables is in terms of path diagrams. Path models for the three data sets just described, with the strength of significant connections represented by standardized regression coefficients, are illustrated in Figure 3.13. Four points should be emphasized regarding these diagrams. First, there are no direct links between age and cognition, and instead all of the age–cognition relations are mediated through the speed variables. This is consistent with the findings illustrated in Figure 3.6

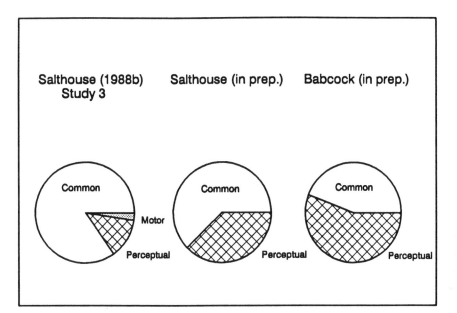

FIGURE 3.12 Venn diagrams illustrating the relative proportion of the variance shared among age, cognition, and speed that is unique to motor speed and to perceptual speed and that is common to both.

that the age–cognition relations were greatly attenuated when an index of speed was statistically controlled.

Second, there is a direct link between age and perceptual speed, indicating that not all of the age-related influences on perceptual speed are mediated through motor speed. Stated somewhat differently, the age-related slowing apparent in perceptual speed measures is not simply attributable to sensory or motor factors because significant age relations in measures of perceptual speed are also evident when measures of motor speed are controlled.

Third, there is a moderate-to-large link between perceptual speed and cognition. This indicates that faster performance in perceptual speed tests is associated with better cognitive performance.

And fourth, the links between motor speed and cognition are either non-existent or negative. A negative relation between motor speed and cognition indicates that faster motor speed is associated with lower levels of cognitive performance. This is opposite to the direction of the perceptual speed influence, and hence it provides additional sup-

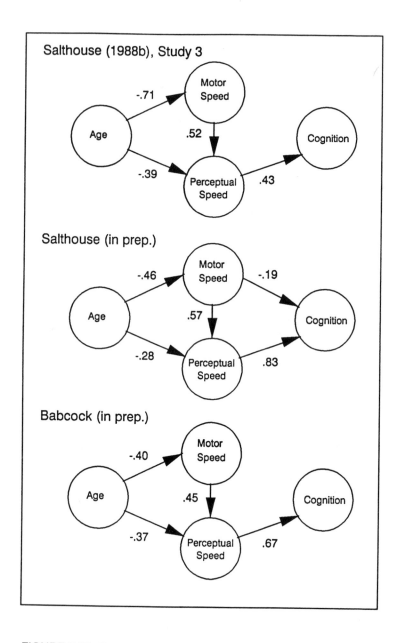

FIGURE 3.13 Path diagrams illustrating significant regression coefficients among age, motor speed, perceptual speed, and cognition.

port for the view that it is perceptual rather than motor speed that is primarily involved in mediating the negative relations between age and cognition. Both the commonality analyses and the path analyses therefore indicate that the most important aspect of speed involved in age–cognition relations is not motoric, although motor speed clearly contributes to the relations between age and perceptual speed.

FURTHER DECOMPOSITION OF SPEED?

Let me briefly summarize the interpretation I am proposing. I have suggested that age–cognition relations might be interpreted in terms of a relation between age and working memory, and that the relation between age and working memory might be explained in terms of a relation between age and speed. A natural question to ask at this time is: What is responsible for the relations between age and speed? That is, what factors, either extrinsic or intrinsic to the organism, lead to the negative relation between age and various measures of speed?

Unfortunately, I am unable to provide an answer to this question at the current time, and in fact I am not sure that a complete answer can be expected solely on the basis of psychological research. I believe that it is likely that understanding of the causes and consequences of age-related variations in processing speed will increase as a greater number of variables are investigated, and as the speed construct becomes more refined and differentiated from other constructs such as attention and arousal. Structural equation modeling is a promising method for this type of research, as long as the importance of cross-validation in independent samples is not neglected. Although results from this kind of research will undoubtedly prove informative, I am not confident that research of this nature will provide a completely satisfactory explanation for why the speed of many variables appears to become slower with increased age.

Because speed of behavior seems to reflect the efficiency of the central nervous system, it is reasonable to speculate that, whatever their distal causes, neurophysiological mechanisms are responsible for age-related slowing. A large number of speculations have been offered, but I am not yet convinced that the alternatives can be distinguished on the basis of behavioral observations and psychological methods of investigation. For example, two major categories of neurophysiological hypotheses are that with increased age there is a slower speed of transmission along single (e.g., loss of myelination) or multiple (e.g., loss of functional cells dictating circuitous linkages) pathways, or that there is delayed propagation at the connections between neural units (e.g., impairment in functioning of neurotransmitters, reduced synchronization of activation patterns). At a somewhat higher level of abstraction, Welford (e.g., 1958) has argued that if neural signals are less distinct or the amount of background noise is higher, then more time will be needed in the older nervous system to achieve a signal-to-noise ratio equivalent to that in the young nervous system. All of these speculations have some plausibility, but it remains to be determined whether they can be distinguished on the basis of observations of behavior without a large number of assumptions, which may themselves not be verifiable from behavior. At the present time, therefore, I view age-related slowing as a potential disciplinary primitive. By this I mean that it is a concept at the boundary of the discipline, and hence it may not be completely decomposable or explainable with the methodological tools of psychology.

It should be emphasized, however, that speed is a unique primitive because it may function like the Rosetta Stone, linking "languages" of different disciplines (Salthouse, 1985b). Unlike other dependent variables in psychology (such as accuracy, solution quality, etc.), time is objectively measurable in a ratio scale, and it has the same meaning across all disciplines. It therefore holds considerable promise as a construct that could integrate research in psychology and neurophysiology.

Chapter 4
Summary

Figure 4.1 represents the best answer I can provide at the current time to the question of what mechanisms are responsible for age–cognition relations. Increased age has been found to be associated with large reductions in both motor speed and perceptual speed, with the effects on the latter at least partially independent of the effects on the former. Slower processing speed, as indexed by measures of perceptual speed, appears to be a direct proximal mediator of poor performance on simple cognitive tests with low levels of item difficulty. Processing speed is hypothesized to affect performance on complex cognitive tests because it contributes to impaired working memory by slowing the rate at which information is activated, and effectively restricting the amount of simultaneously available information during the solution process. This interpretation obviously is incomplete because many age-related influences on cognition are still not understood, particularly those represented by the dotted lines in the figure, and no explanation is available yet for why increased age is associated with slower motor and perceptual speed.

It is important to emphasize that I am not claiming that all age-related effects on cognition are attributable to influences of processing speed and working memory. Instead, I am merely suggesting that these appear to be important factors that are associated with, and hence may be contributing to, the adult age differences in a range of cognitive measures. The discovery that measures of perceptual speed are associated with a large proportion of the age-related variance in a variety of cognitive measures indicates that slower speed is a characteristic closely related to the lower levels of cognitive performance associated with increased age. Much research still needs to be done to identify the true causal variables, but on the basis of the available evidence it appears very likely that processing speed will be found to be involved

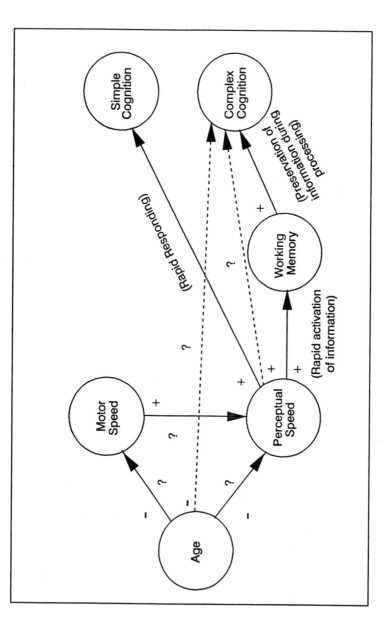

FIGURE 4.1 Provisional answer to the question of what mechanisms are responsible for age–cognition relations. The pluses and minuses indicate the direction of the relation, question marks indicate that the mechanisms have not yet been identified, and relations with dashed lines are suspected but not yet confirmed.

in the causal relations between age and fluid or processing efficiency aspects of cognition.

There is often a tendency to characterize theoretical positions in extremes, and for proponents to consider an interpretation as successful if it can account for some results, and for critics to consider it as unsuccessful if it can't account for all potentially relevant results. I believe that it is much more reasonable to evaluate potential interpretations in terms of how much they can explain, either with respect to the number of variables encompassed within the interpretation, or in terms of the proportion of age-related variance accounted for in a given variable. The research described in the previous chapters suggests that the influences of working memory and processing speed are fairly impressive with both of these criteria. Working memory and processing speed appear to be involved in the age differences on a wide variety of variables, and with some variables they have been found to be associated with as much as 50% to 90% of the age-related variance. Some of the causal linkages are still quite speculative, but the evidence that working memory and processing speed are involved as important proximal mediators of the relations between age and cognition now seems reasonably strong.

DIRECTIONS FOR FUTURE RESEARCH

What type of research should be conducted to extend these ideas? At least two important directions for future research can be identified based on the empirical evidence and interpretations presented in the preceding chapters. One direction for future research is to determine the causes of the hypothesized broad or general factors, and to extend the investigation of the mechanisms by which they operate. If, as the evidence seems to suggest, relatively general factors like processing speed and working memory are associated with a large proportion of the age differences in a variety of different cognitive tasks, then it obviously is important to determine why and how these relations exist.

The causes of the age differences in working memory and processing speed need to be investigated because, as noted in chapter 1, there is a sense in which proximal process-related mediators are merely refined descriptions of what needs to be explained. If it is really the case that a large proportion of the age-related differences in cognition can be accounted for in terms of differences in these processing characteristics, then a great reduction has been achieved in the number of phenomena in need of explanation. Ultimately, however, the distal determinants of these proximal characteristics must be identified and isolated.

Another high priority within the thematic focus on causes of the hypothesized mediators is to clarify exactly what is meant by the constructs of working memory and processing speed. Of particular concern in this respect is avoiding both reification of the constructs by unquestioning acceptance of the belief that a thing exists merely because it has a name, and the tendency to invoke a label as an explanation. In order for the speculations to evolve into a genuine explanation, the constructs of processing speed and working memory must be refined and elaborated, and mechanisms specified (and investigated) for how they affect cognitive functioning, and how they are affected by factors related to increased age.

The range of influence of these mediators also needs to be explored by systematically investigating different types of cognitive variables. In effect, therefore, the construct of cognition also has to be refined, and perhaps differentiated into coherent subclassifications on the basis of susceptibility to various types of age-related influences. This is desirable if for no other reason than that it may be implausible to expect that mediators have the same magnitude of influence, and operate according to the same mechanisms, with all cognitive variables.

A second important direction for future research concerns the distinction between general and specific age-related influences on cognition, and how this distinction is best operationalized. Although it could be argued that the fastest progress in understanding cognitive aging phenomena will be achieved by concentrating on the broadest and most general influences, there is still a need to investigate age-related effects that are presumed to be specific to limited sets of variables. However, even in the investigation of specific interpretations of cognitive aging phenomena it is important to be sensitive to the possibility that there may be influences of relatively general factors like working memory and speed of processing. That is, instead of postulating a null hypothesis of no age differences that keeps getting rejected, it may be more productive to start with the hypothesis of one or more general influences, and then to try to determine when, and why, the general influences are not sufficient to account for the observed differences. A strategy of this type seems justified because cumulative progress in the explanation of cognitive aging effects will occur only by acknowledging the relevant factors that have already been identified. This doesn't mean that those factors are necessarily understood, but merely that a causal influence for which considerable evidence currently exists should not be ignored when attempting to explain the age-related effects apparent on a particular cognitive variable.

It therefore may be reasonable to focus on specific interpretations only after the necessity of such interpretations has been clearly established, perhaps by demonstrating that the results deviate significantly from what would be expected from any general influences that might be operating. This suggestion does not mean that analytical research oriented toward specific interpretations of age-related differences in measures of cognitive functioning should be abandoned, but rather that it should be pursued only after first removing the influence of any potentially more general factors that have already been identified (see Salthouse, in press-e).

The major question that arises in light of this recommendation is how general and specific age-related influences are best distinguished. The simplest method at the present time seems to involve the use of statistical control procedures. That is, researchers might routinely include several measures of processing speed (and possibly working memory) in their studies, and then use techniques like multiple regression to remove the influence of these variables before conducting analyses of specific age-related effects on the residual scores. Although this appears to be the easiest and best understood technique currently available, regression-based procedures are not without limitations. Other techniques therefore need to be explored to identify variables sharing similar causes of age-related differences. Because distinguishing between general and specific age-related influences appears to be a major obstacle hampering progress in understanding age–cognition relations, a high priority for future research should be the identification of suitable investigative procedures, and the application of those procedures to as many data sets as possible.

CONCLUDING COMMENTS

Are we any closer to explaining why increased age is often associated with lower levels of performance in many measures of cognitive functioning? Although the relevant phenomena have not yet been adequately explained, I believe that results of the type described in the preceding chapters have contributed to greater knowledge of the mechanisms involved in age–cognition relations. This point can be illustrated by contrasting Figures 1.1 and 4.1. Not only does the latter figure contain more hypothesized mechanisms, but the unexplained relations are much more specific. The mere fact that the questions are becoming more precise and focused thus can be viewed as an indication that progress is indeed occurring in the understanding of the relations between age and cognition.

References

Babcock, R. L. (in preparation). *Analysis of adult age differences on the Raven's Advanced Progressive Matrices Test*. Doctoral dissertation, Georgia Institute of Technology.

Babcock, R. L., & Salthouse, T. A. (1990). Effects of increased processing demands on age differences in working memory. *Psychology and Aging, 5,* 421–428.

Baddeley, A. D., & Hitch, G. J. (1974). Working Memory. In G.A. Bower (Ed.), *The psychology of learning and motivation* (Vol. 8, pp. 47–90). New York: Academic Press.

Birren, J. E. (1974). Translations in gerontology—From lab to life: Psychophysiology and speed of response. *American Psychologist, 29,* 808–815.

Broadbent, D. E. (1971). *Decision and stress*. London: Academic Press.

Cerella, J. (1985). Information processing rates in the elderly. *Psychological Bulletin, 98,* 67–83.

Cohen, J. (1988). *Statistical power analysis for the behavioral sciences* (2nd ed.), Hillsdale, NJ: Lawrence Erlbaum Associates, Inc.

Daneman, M., & Carpenter, P. A. (1980). Individual differences in working memory and reading. *Journal of Verbal Learning and Verbal Behavior, 19,* 450–466.

Eysenck, H. J. (1987). Speed of information processing, reaction time, and the theory of intelligence. In P. A. Vernon (Ed.), *Speed of information processing and intelligence* (pp. 21–67). Norwood, NJ: Ablex.

Ghiselli, E. E. (1973). The validity of aptitude tests in personnel selection. *Personnel Psychology, 26,* 461–477.

Hertzog, C. (1989). Influences of cognitive slowing on age differences in intelligence. *Developmental Psychology, 25,* 636–651.

Horn, J. L., & Cattell, R. B. (1967). Age differences in fluid and crystallized intelligence. *Acta Psychologica, 26,* 107–129.

Hunter, J. E., & Hunter, R. F. (1984). Validity and utility of alternative predictors of job performance. *Psychological Bulletin, 93,* 328–367.

Jensen, A. R. (1987). Individual differences in the Hick paradigm. In P. A. Vernon (Ed.), *Speed of information processing and intelligence* (pp. 101–175). Norwood, NJ: Ablex.

Kaufman, A. S. (1990). *Assessing adolescent and adult intelligence*. Boston: Allyn & Bacon.

Lemmon, V. W. (1927). The relation of reaction time to measures of intelligence, memory, and learning. *Archives of Psychology* (Whole No. 94).

Pedhazur, E. J. (1982). *Multiple regression in behavioral research*. New York: Holt, Rinehart & Winston.

Salthouse, T. A. (1980). Age and memory: Strategies for localizing the loss. In L. W.

Poon, J. L. Fozard, L. Cermak, D. Arenberg, & L. W. Thompson (Eds.), *New directions in memory and aging* (pp. 47–65). Hillsdale, NJ: Lawrence Erlbaum Associates, Inc.

Salthouse, T. A. (1985a). Speed of behavior and its implications for cognition. In J. E. Birren & K. W. Schaie (Eds.), *Handbook of the psychology of aging* (2nd ed., pp. 400–426). New York: Van Nostrand Reinhold.

Salthouse, T. A. (1985b). *A theory of cognitive aging.* Amsterdam: North-Holland.

Salthouse, T. A. (1987a). Adult age differences in integrative spatial ability. *Psychology and Aging, 2,* 254–260.

Salthouse, T. A. (1987b). Sources of age-related individual differences in block design tasks. *Intelligence, 11,* 245–262.

Salthouse, T. A. (1987c). The role of representations in age differences in analogical reasoning. *Psychology and Aging, 2,* 357–362.

Salthouse, T. A. (1988a). Resource-reduction interpretations of cognitive aging. *Developmental Review, 8,* 238–272.

Salthouse, T. A. (1988b). The role of processing resources in cognitive aging. In M. L. Howe & C. J. Brainerd (Eds.), *Cognitive development in adulthood* (pp. 185–239). New York: Springer-Verlag.

Salthouse, T. A. (1988c). The complexity of Age × Complexity functions: Comment on Charness and Campbell. *Journal of Experimental Psychology: General, 117,* 425–428.

Salthouse, T. A. (1990). Working memory as a processing resource in cognitive aging. *Developmental Review, 10,* 101–124.

Salthouse, T. A. (1991a). Mediation of adult age differences in cognition by reductions in working memory and speed of processing. *Psychological Science, 2,* 179–183.

Salthouse, T. A. (1991b). *Theoretical perspectives on cognitive aging.* Hillsdale, NJ: Lawrence Erlbaum Associates, Inc.

Salthouse, T. A. (1991c). Age and experience effects on the interpretation of orthographic drawings of three-dimensional objects. *Psychology and Aging, 6,* 426–433.

Salthouse (in press-a). Influence of processing speed on adult age differences in working memory. *Acta Psychologica.*

Salthouse, T. A. (in press-b). What do adult age differences in Digit Symbol reflect? *Journal of Gerontology: Psychological Sciences.*

Salthouse, T. A. (in press-c). Why do adult age differences increase with task complexity? *Developmental Psychology.*

Salthouse, T. A. (in press-d). Working-memory mediation of adult age differences in integrative reasoning. *Memory & Cognition.*

Salthouse, T. A. (in press-e). Shifting levels of analysis in the understanding of cognitive aging. *Human Development.*

Salthouse, T. A. (under review). *Influence of working memory on adult age differences in matrix reasoning.*

Salthouse, T. A. (in preparation). *Speed mediation of adult age differences in cognition.*

Salthouse, T. A. & Babcock, R. L. (1991). Decomposing adult age differences in working memory. *Developmental Psychology, 27,* 763–776.

Salthouse, T. A., Babcock, R. L., & Shaw, R. J. (1991). Effects of adult age on structural and operational capacities in working memory. *Psychology and Aging, 6,* 118–127.

Salthouse, T. A., Babcock, R. L., Skovronek, E., Mitchell, D. R. D., & Palmon, R. (1990). Age and experience effects in spatial visualization. *Developmental Psychology, 26,* 128–136.

Salthouse, T. A., Kausler, D. H., & Saults, J. S. (1988). Utilization of path analytic procedures to investigate the role of processing resources in cognitive aging. *Psychology and Aging, 3,* 158–166.

Salthouse, T. A., Kausler, D. H., & Saults, J. S. (1990). Age, self-assessed health status, and cognition. *Journal of Gerontology: Psychological Sciences, 45,* P156–P160.

Salthouse, T. A., & Mitchell, D. R. D. (1989). Structural and operational capacities in integrative spatial ability. *Psychology and Aging, 4,* 18–25.

Salthouse, T. A., & Mitchell, D. R. D. (1990). Effects of age and naturally occurring experience on spatial visualization performance. *Developmental Psychology, 26,* 845–854.

Salthouse, T. A., Mitchell, D. R. D., & Palmon, R. (1989). Memory and age differences in spatial manipulation ability. *Psychology and Aging, 4,* 480–486.

Salthouse, T. A., Mitchell, D. R. D., Skovronek, E., & Babcock, R. L. (1989). Effects of adult age and working memory on reasoning and spatial abilities. *Journal of Experimental Psychology: Learning, Memory, and Cognition, 15,* 507–516.

Salthouse, T. A., & Prill, K. A. (1987). Inferences about age impairments in inferential reasoning. *Psychology and Aging, 2,* 43–51.

Salthouse, T. A., & Skovronek, E. (in press). Within-context assessment of age differences in working memory. *Journal of Gerontology: Psychological Sciences.*

Salthouse, T. A., & Somberg, B. (1982a). Skilled performance: Effects of adult age and experience on elementary processes. *Journal of Experimental Psychology: General, 111,* 176–207.

Salthouse, T. A., & Somberg, B. (1982b). Time–accuracy relationships in young and old adults. *Journal of Gerontology, 37,* 349–353.

Schaie, K. W. (1985). *The Schaie–Thurstone Adult Mental Abilities Test.* Palo Alto, CA: Consulting Psychologists Press.

Schaie, K. W. (1989). Perceptual speed in adulthood: Cross-sectional and longitudinal studies. *Psychology and Aging, 4,* 443–453.

Vernon, P. A. (1987). New developments in reaction time research. In P. A. Vernon (Ed.), *Speed of information processing and intelligence* (pp. 1–20). Norwood, NJ: Ablex.

Wechsler, D. (1981). *Manual for the Wechsler Adult Intelligence Scale–Revised.* New York: The Psychological Corporation.

Welford, A. T. (1958). *Ageing and human skill.* London: Oxford University Press.

Author Index

Babcock, R. L., 32, 42, 43, 46, 54, 73, 76, 79, 112, *125, 127*
Baddeley, A. D., 40, *125*
Birren, J. E., 83, *125*
Broadbent, D. E., 40, *125*
Carpenter, P. A., 40, *125*
Cattell, R. B., *125*
Cerella, J., 106, *125*
Cohen, J., 12, *125*
Daneman, M., 40, *125*
Eysenck, H. J. 83, *125*
Ghiselli, E., 14, *125*
Hertzog, C., 93, 110, *125*
Hitch, G. J., 40, *125*
Horn, J. L., 3, *125*
Hunter, J. E., 14, *125*
Hunter, R. F., 14, *125*
Jensen, A. R., 83, *125*
Kaufman, A. S., 13, 14, *125*
Kausler, D. H., 7, 10, 11, 33, 94, *127*

Lemmon, V. W., 83, 84, *125*
Mitchell, D. R. D., 7, 9, 31, 32, 46, 54, 63, 68, 70, 72, 94, *127*
Palmon, R., 32, 68, 70, *127*
Pedhazur, E. J., 60, *125*
Prill, K. A., 72, 86, *127*
Salthouse, T. A., 7–11, 16, 17, 23, 29–33, 39, 42, 43, 45–47, 50, 54, 59, 63, 68,79, 70–73, 76, 83–86, 91–96, 98–99, 104, 107, 109, 111, 116, 123, *125, 126, 127*
Saults, J. S., 7. 10, 11, 33, *127*
Schaie, K. W., 93, 95, 110, *127*
Shaw, R. J., 76, 79, *127*
Skovronek, E., 32, 46, 50, 54, 70, 71, *127*
Somberg, B., 84, 85, *127*
Vernon, P. A., 83, *127*
Wechsler, D., 3, 13, 14, 89, *127*
Welford, A. T., 39, 116, *127*

Subject Index

Age
  meaning of, 20
Age-complexity effects, 48, 52, 54
Age differences
  general and specific, 122–123
  independence of, 16–17, 101
Backwards Digit Span, 45–46, 76
Block design, 85
Calendar Test, 96
Commonality analyses, 60–62, 111
Complex cognitive performance, 59–61
Composite measures, 19, 45–46, 50
Computation span, 41–46, 60, 71, 73–74
Cube Assembly Test, 46, 59, 62
Cube Comparison Test, 48–50, 70–71
Digit Symbol Substitution Test, 76, 89, 91–95,
  111
Disuse, 30
Education, 4, 30–31
Experience, 30–32
Experimental analysis, 20, 29, 71
Figure Classification Test, 96
Finding As Test, 94
Following Directions Test, 96
Geometric Analogies Test, 45–46, 50–52, 59,
  62, 93–94, 111
Health status, 33–34
Identical Pictures Test, 96
Information availability, 61–72
Integrative reasoning, 46, 54–55, 57, 59, 62–66,
  68–69
Intelligence, 3
Letter Sets Test, 94, 96
Line span, 42, 71
Listening span, 41–46, 60, 73–74

Matrix reasoning, 58, 66–68, 71, 98
Mediation
  direct and indirect, 21
  mechanisms, 122
Mediator, 20–22, 26, 29
  distal, 30–32
  etiology, 23–24
  importance, 24–25
  process-related, 34–35, 121–122
  proximal, 33–35
  types, 29–30, 33
Memory, 98–99
  spatial, 11, 31, 34
  verbal, 11, 31, 34
Mental synthesis, 45, 52–54, 68, 70, 93–94, 111
Method of systematic relations, 101–110
Motor speed, 111–115
Number Comparison Test, 94, 96
Number Series Completion Test, 86, 94
Occupation, 12–14
Paired Associates Test, 11, 31, 34, 98
Paper Folding Test, 5, 7–9, 11, 31, 34, 45–46,
  54–56, 58–59, 62–65, 93–94
Path diagrams, 112–115, 119–120
Perceptual speed, 76, 88–92, 111–115
Processing speed, 83
  and practice, 84–85
  and speed–accuracy tradeoff, 85–86
  general versus specific, 100–102, 106–108,
    110
  measures of, 88–92
  speculations about, 99–100, 115–116
  statistical control of, 93–99
Raven's Progressive Matrices Test, 5–8, 11, 31,
  34, 46, 66, 95–96

Recognition probes, 66–71
Redundant information requests, 71
Reliability, 27
Replication, 19, 29
Sample size, 26–27
Schaie–Thurstone Tests, 95
Shipley Abstraction Test, 11, 31, 34, 46, 94–95
Spatial Matrix Memory Test, 5, 7, 10
Speed factors, 86–88, 111
Standard deviations, 7, 14–15
Statistical control, 20–24, 29, 43–44, 61
     methodological requirements of, 26–28
Surface Development Test, 11, 31, 34, 94
Symbol Copying Test, 111
Validity, 14, 27–28

Variance, 18
     age-related, 11, 17, 24–26, 43–44, 46, 59–
          60, 75–76, 92, 94–96, 98, 121
     proportion of, 7, 11–12, 25, 43–44
Venn diagram, 7, 11, 24–26, 60, 113
WAIS–R3, 13–14
Working memory
     as mediator, 40
     definition, 39
     demands, 48–59
     desktop metaphor, 72–73
     juggling metaphor, 77, 79
     measurement of, 40–42, 45
     speed and, 76–79
     statistical control of, 46–48